The Composition of Herman Melville

Rick Mitchell

intellect™
Bristol, UK
Portland, OR, USA

This Edition Published in UK in 2002 by
Intellect Books, PO Box 862, Bristol BS99 1DE, UK

This Edition Published in USA in 2002 by
Intellect Books, ISBS, 5824 N.E. Hassalo St, Portland, Oregon 97213-3644, USA

Consulting Editor:	Peter Thomson
Cover Design	Roger Magowan
Copy Editor:	Holly Spradling

A catalogue record for this book is available from the British Library

ISBN 1-84150-067-4

This book is also published to be a supplement to Mitchell, R., 'Composing Herman Melville: performing history through the presence of the now' in *Studies in Theatre and Performance* vol 21 no 2 (Intellect, 2001).

Printed and bound in Great Britain by 4edge Ltd, Hockley. www.4edge.co.uk

Author

Rick Mitchell, whose plays include *Urban Renewal, Potlatch, Cruising the Caribbean Old Pleasures in the New World,* and *American Labor*, teaches playwriting, drama and performance in the Department of English at California State University, Northridge. Formerly, Mitchell made his living as a professional comedian and ventriloquist, working throughout the USA, the Caribbean, and on television. Mitchell's latest play is *Brecht in L.A.*.

Dedication

to my son and daughter
Christopher Ryan and Emily Caroline

Acknowledgements

California State University, Northridge has provided generous support for *The Composition of Herman Melville.* I would especially like to thank Dr. Mack I. Johnson, Associate Vice-President, Graduate Studies, Research and International Programs; Dr. Jorge Garcia, Dean, College of Humanities; and Dr. Robert Noreen, Chair, Department of English, for helping me to see this project through to completion. And I'm grateful to Darrell Bourque and Joe Andriano for their perceptive comments on the text, to Bob Russett for his invaluable ideas about the play's visual elements, and to Roger Magowan for doing the cover design at such a late stage.

I would also like to thank Caroline for her expert direction, astonishingly effective performances, and - when required - engaged spectatorship during the everyday, as well as for her (usually) patient tolerance of my Melvillean writing habits. And I'd like to thank my students at Cal State, Northridge for constantly reminding me - through inspired performances of their own texts - that playwriting and theatre must remain, first and foremost, fun.

Explanatory Notes

The Characters

The play can be performed with a minimum of six actors.

Herman Melville (an author)

Lizzie Melville (wife of Herman)

Chief Justice Lemuel Shaw (father of Lizzie)

The Cosmopolitan (dark-skinned male)

He performs the following five roles, but never himself:

Flaneur
Boy
Freak (freak exhibit)
Character
Simpson (escaped slave)

Young Mackie (son of Lizzie and Herman; a boy)

Mackie (Young Mackie as an adolescent, 17-18 yrs. old)

Jameson (an Irishman)

Virgil (a ventriloquist)

Dummy (a dark-skinned ventriloquial figure)

Savage (played by the ventriloquial figure)

Stanwix (off-stage; child.)

Elizabeth (off-stage; child)

Actor #2

Spectator (non-speaking role)

Note– *one actor can play all of the following roles.*

Scholar
Actor
Actor #1
Hawker (hawks books, newspapers)
Rantaul (attorney representing Simpson)
Reverend (presides over funeral)
Cop
Lincoln (the U.S. President)
Photographer

Setting

The play, set primarily in the U.S. in the mid-nineteenth century, calls for a fluid, somewhat abstract set.

Acts/Scenes

The plays consists of two acts, thirty-one scenes, a prologue, and an epilogue.

Notes on Casting

As indicated above, one actor can play the last nine characters. Also, it is possible to have one person, a male or female, play both Mackie (a young boy) and Young Mackie (Mackie as an eighteen year old); to have the actor playing Shaw also play Jameson; and to utilize actors cast in other roles to also play the minor roles of Hawker, Virgil, Stanwix, Elizabeth, Actor #2, and Spectator. Such casting would enable the play to be produced with six actors. Unless specificed, the characters in the play do not necessarily have to be played by actors of any particular race. When casting, consider utilizing actors of color to play some of the characters (e.g. Lizzie, Judge Lemuel Shaw) based on historical figures who were white.

General Notes

The overall pace of this play must be quick, with little if any downtime in between scenes. In addition to writing text often, characters sometimes read text aloud (which will help to emphasize the act of composition—a central theme of the play), and two or more actions should often take place simultaneously, even when not specified in the script. For example, during a scene between Lizzie and Shaw, Melville could be working maniacally at his desk on another part of the stage, or Lizzie could be copying one of Melville's manuscripts at her desk as Melville appears in another scene with Mackie. Also, Melville loves the words that he writes, and this should be apparent when he reads and/or recites words from his texts. Although the script specifies at times that certain characters are speaking offstage and/or on a large video screen (or on a video wall comprised of numerous monitors), or that there are certain light changes (lighting directions are often omitted), you may choose to alter these particular stage directions at times. (If you do not use video during the production, consider using slide projections and/or a back-lit scrim at times.) Throughout performances that incorporate video there should be a rich and continuous montage of images, and the images on the video screen should at times be antithetical to previous and following images, and to the play itself. (Avoid using images that are uninteresting in themselves, or too literal.) Such an approach to imagery may help to create what Sergei Eisenstein calls a montage "collision" between the video images themselves, as well as between these images and the stage "images." During performances that utilize video, a video-camera operator, who might be played by one or more of the actors, should also be on-stage in order to transmit closed-circuit images at times, and the main characters—except for Melville—should periodically glance at the video screen, which provokes within them fear and, increasingly, seductive awe. (Towards the end of productions that utilize video, Mackie should glance at the video screen for increasingly long periods.)

Brief Notes about the Set, etc.

The set should be somewhat abstract—and practical—so that the action can remain fluid, especially in between scenes and during simultaneous scenes. Pages of text—

including fragments from the play, Melville's *oeuvre*, and other sources—should hang above the stage. If the production utilizes video, the video apparatus may also display text, as well as the ocean, which can wash over and away from various other images. Outmoded technology, such as candles and fuel-based lamps, can share the performance space with modern technology, such as video monitors, and the outmoded technology on the stage may at times also be seen for prolonged periods on individual video monitors. And the following words may appear periodically: EVERY EPOCH DREAMS ITS SUCCESSOR. In one part of the performance space an oil-fuelled lamp burns on an old desk upon which Lizzie often transcribes Melville's virtually unreadable handwritten manuscripts into fair copy for publication. As she continues this action throughout the performance, an enormous (and exaggerated) amount of paper slowly piles up on both the desk and the floor. Perhaps an electric fan can scatter the paper around the area of her desk. Throughout the play Melville is working at his own desk (which is in a different part of the performance space), reading from numerous books and often writing (while sitting, standing, leaning on the desk) voraciously. The audience should see Melville and Lizzie working at their desks often, even during scenes in which they do not appear. Additionally, music should accompany the songs, as well as various other parts of the play, and throughout the performance sheets of writing paper may periodically float down from above.

Notes on Projections

Throughout the script, various projections of words and images are indicated. If a video wall is being used, the words and imagery will not be projections but direct video images. Below, please find various textual projections (or video images) that should be presented during the course of the play. Although various publication dates are given, feel free to omit some of these dates. (In order to strengthen the play's dramatic elements, the playwright sometimes takes poetic license with historical "facts," both verifiable and unverifiable, so the publication dates do not always match up with what's going on in the play.) While you might choose to spread the projections of the titles of Melville's books throughout the play, perhaps omitting such projections during Melville's unproductive periods, you could also run the projections close together at times and even repeat them in order to emphasize Melville's intense engagement with the written word. Following are the projections: *Typee: A Peep at Polynesian Life*, published 1846; *Omoo: A Narrative of Adventures in the South Seas*, published 1847; *Mardi and a Voyage Thither*, published 1849; *White-Jacket or The World in a Man-of-War*, published 1850; *Moby-Dick or The Whale*, published 1851; *Pierre or The Ambiguities*, published 1852; Short stories, published 1853-1854; *Israel Potter: His Fifty Years of Exile*, published 1855; *The Piazza Tales*, published 1856; *The Confidence-Man: His Masquerade*, published 1857; *Battle-Pieces and Aspects of the War*, published 1866; *Clarel: A Poem and Pilgrimage in the Holy Land*, published privately 1876; *John Marr and Other Sailors*, published privately 1888; *Timoleon*, published privately 1891.

ACT ONE

Prologue

SCHOLAR *(SCHOLAR stands in the dark at a lectern dreamily staring off into space. His elbow leans on the lectern, and his head rests on his hand. Suddenly, a spotlight's beam jolts him from his daydream.)* Oh... *(Looks at watch, tries to look alert.)* I...I thought I had some more time.... Ummm... *(SCHOLAR smiles, realizes he does not have his written speech.)* Hold on just one second... *(As he walks to the side of the stage an ACTOR hands him his speech. To ACTOR.)* Thank you... *(SCHOLAR returns to lectern, reads in overly pompous tone.)* Now...ladies and gentlemen, eminent scholars...of...the First Annual Melvillean Society Conference... Today... *(He drops first page of speech.)* We, uh... Why don't I just jump ahead a bit? *(He nervously laughs, tries to compose himself, smiles, reads.)* Ummm...perhaps Mr. Melville's literary endeavors were once shunned because his readers stood too closely to the Civil War. But now, with over two decades distance from the end of the nineteenth century, with the horrors of our first and last World War firmly behind us, Americans can finally appreciate Mr. Melville's rhapsodically sublime vision... As mankind makes unprecedented advances away from the vulgarities of war, savagery... *(He drops page, picks it up, reads.)* Ummm...*idiocy*...and finds time for the placid contemplation of Art, I predict that Mr. Melville's stature will grow ex...exponentially. And seventy-six years from now, after America has reached a pinnacle of perfection of which today we cannot even dream, Herman Melville's *oeuvre* will be recognized as the most timeless and universal example of literature ever to set it roots deep down into the soul, uh...soil...of these United States. *(pause)* Thank you... *(ACTOR hands SCHOLAR a note, which the latter scans. SCHOLAR then picks up from the lectern a pistol with which he's intrigued, unthinkingly waves gun, points it at audience, chuckles. He reads note.)* Oh... If you haven't done so already, please make sure that you visit our Melville memorabilia exhibit, where you can catch a rare glimpse of authentic items, including this antique firearm used by Mr. Melville's son, Mackie. Also, as we've been... *(The note seems to have come to an end. SCHOLAR nervously looks up, from side to side.)* Well...

ACTOR. *(From off-stage.)* Turn it over.

SCHOLAR *(SCHOLAR turns over note, reads.)* As we've been announcing all week, we will now present our special entertainment... And please remain after the...the conclusion of the play for an important announcement of a startling discovery of a lost work by Mr. Melville... *(pause)* Thank you. *(Light applause. SCHOLAR EXITS.)*

The Composition of Herman Melville

Scene One

(JUDGE LEMUEL SHAW'S parlor. Boston, Massachusetts.)

SHAW *(SHAW reads the following passage from Typee with a critical tone. Projection: TYPEE: A PEEP AT POLYNESIAN LIFE, by Herman Melville. LIZZIE softly plays the piano.)* No sooner are the images overturned, the temples demolished, and the idolaters converted into *nominal* Christians, than disease, vice, and premature death make their appearance. The depopulated land is then recruited from the rapacious hordes of enlightened individuals who settle themselves within its borders, and clamorously announce the progress of Truth. Neat villas, trim gardens, shaven lawns, spires, and cupolas arise—

LIZZIE Come on, Herman. *(LIZZIE plays the piano more loudly.)*

SHAW While the poor savage soon finds himself an interloper in the country of his fathers.

MELVILLE *("Song of the Heathen Queen.")*

'Tis dark where strays my heathen dear,
Why does she from me roam?
For well she knows my heart is drear,
As I sail on this ship, my home.
But what soft music greets mine ear,
What strain comes o'er the dell?
Such sweetness to me, the nightwinds bear,
That sound, her savage yell.
Oh send the boat to the queen of night,
Who glides through sparkling mountain trails.
And spreads her finest robes of light,
To guide her through the dewey dales.
She comes, she comes, her voice I hear,
Her pretty form I see.
Oh soon they'll bear my heathen dear,
In joy again to me.
Oh soon they'll bear my heathen dear,
In joy again to me.
(SHAW applauds.)

LIZZIE *(To MELVILLE.)*Did I get it right that time?

MELVILLE Almost perfect, Lizzie.

SHAW You ought to put a stage show together, Herman.

MELVILLE I'm not much of a performer.

SHAW You're always performing. Sailor songs, whaling tales—

MELVILLE I'd rather just concentrate on my writing.

SHAW Look at that Englishman with the tattoos, umm... Matthews... (*SHAW imitates a sidewalk barker.)* John F. Matthews, the celebrated tattooed man. Held six years in savage captivity. In a drama of his life.

LIZZIE *Typee's* been selling quite well.

SHAW Herman could sell a hundred times as many copies if he had his own stage show. *(To HERMAN.)* And you wouldn't even have to write the show out. You could just tell the audience the same stories you're always telling us. About Fayaway, the savage princess... Karky, the cannibal artist... Sing a few of your sea shanties.

LIZZIE Herman's doing perfectly well with his novels.

SHAW Well, he was...at least with the one that's been published.

LIZZIE *Omoo* is going to be even better.

SHAW (*Imitating a cow.*) O-moooooo...

LIZZIE I wouldn't be surprised if it sells out.

SHAW O-moooooo... (*SHAW laughs.)*

LIZZIE I think the title's kind of catchy.

SHAW Yeah, for a bottle of milk. (*SHAW laughs.)*

LIZZIE Omoo's from the Polynesian—

SHAW *(To MELVILLE.)* You're not dedicating *this* novel to me, are you?

MELVILLE No.

SHAW Now don't get me wrong, I think *Typee's* an extraordinary book. And a bit deeper, of course, than the pamphlet by the tattooed Englishman.

MELVILLE I should hope so—

SHAW Although there are some parallels.

LIZZIE Herman writes literature, father.

SHAW In both of the stories the protagonist jumps a whaling ship in the South Seas, he's held captive...escapes...

MELVILLE Matthews's pamphlet's not worth the paper it's printed on.

SHAW Of course your work is much more literate, but that's not the reason people were buying it.

LIZZIE There are some intelligent people who read *Typee*—

SHAW Americans want adventure, not philosophy.

MELVILLE If I only gave readers what they desired to hear, why then I'd—

SHAW You'd be very popular.

LIZZIE That's not why Herman's an author.

SHAW You know, it was bad enough when people started questioning the book's veracity as a travel narrative. But now with several prominent religious leaders, right here in Boston, up in arms about what *they* consider to be a heathenish book...a work of the devil himself—

MELVILLE (*MELVILLE laughs.*) That's really pushing it, sir.

SHAW I know, it's ludicrous.

LIZZIE They haven't even read it.

SHAW But if people are thinking that way about a novel, regardless of whether they're right or wrong—and my name's attached to it—then anyone can just pick up the book, quote certain passages, and say that Judge Lemuel Shaw, the Chief Justice of the Massachusetts Supreme Court, is supportive of abolition, anti-Christian views...

LIZZIE You should be honored that Herman dedicated his first novel to you.

SHAW I am. But if Herman could only take some of the book's more entertaining aspects and put them into a stage show, why then—

MELVILLE I'd get the same response.

SHAW Not if it's entertainment. (*LIZZIE begins to EXIT.*)

MELVILLE Any book has to be entertaining.

SHAW You can still tell your cannibal stories. Americans love that sort of thing. I mean, look at the long lines to get into those exhibits produced by that, uh, showman down in New York...

MELVILLE Barnum.

SHAW P.T. Barnum's making a killing. Off of the same people who are ridiculing your book.

LIZZIE Several critics *do* consider *Typee* a success, father. Herman's second novel's being published... (*LIZZIE EXITS.*)

SHAW Just remember your readers' limitations.

MELVILLE They're certainly capable of thinking.

SHAW I know several attorneys down in New York, Herman—and right here in Boston—that are always looking for a bright, young apprentice who knows how to write. (*LIZZIE ENTERS with a tray of scones.*)

LIZZIE Anyone for fresh scones?

MELVILLE No thank you.

LIZZIE They just came out of the oven. (*SHAW begins to eat a scone.*)

SHAW Don't you think he'd make a fine attorney, Lizzie? Or a judge?

LIZZIE He's much too creative for that.

SHAW But Herman has to find a way to make all of that creativity pay off. And I'm sure that he could. I mean, the tattooed Englishman did it, and he doesn't have half Herman's ability...

MELVILLE I'm going out for a walk. (*MELVILLE abruptly EXITS.*)

LIZZIE What about your coat? *(pause)* Why must you continually devalue Herman's efforts?

SHAW Lizzie, I've known Herman's family since before you were born. I helped Herman's mother out after his father passed away, penniless. And if I think that Maria's son might be able to benefit from some constructive advice...

LIZZIE You were comparing him to the tattooed Englishman.

SHAW To tell you the truth, Lizzie... Well...your stepmother and I think the world of the Melvilles...but we never pictured you with a sailor from a whaling ship.

LIZZIE Herman was just...collecting material.

SHAW There are plenty of eligible men right here in Beacon Hill.

LIZZIE (*Worried.*) Herman doesn't know Boston that well.

SHAW You're very intelligent, you know.

LIZZIE He shouldn't be walking around out there at night—

SHAW The smartest of all your siblings... So I'm sure that you'll make the right—

LIZZIE I'm going to go out there and find him. (*LIZZIE EXITS.*)

Scene Two

(Boston Common.)

(MELVILLE, who feels quite cold, ENTERS. FLANEUR ENTERS from different side of performance space.)

FLANEUR Hello.

MELVILLE Good evening. (*MELVILLE does a double-take.*) We don't know each other...

FLANEUR No.

MELVILLE You look familiar... (*MELVILLE walks.*)

FLANEUR Do you have a cigarette?

MELVILLE *(pause)* Ummm...sure. (*MELVILLE gives FLANEUR a cigarette.*)

FLANEUR Light? (*MELVILLE lights cigarette.*) So what brings you out to Boston Common tonight?

MELVILLE I...I just needed some exercise.

FLANEUR Well, you picked the coldest night of the— *(In the distance, off-stage, JAMESON whistles "Dixie". Whistling slowly increases in volume.)*

MELVILLE I have to take care of my health.

FLANEUR So you're not wearing a coat?

MELVILLE *(pause)* The...the cold doesn't bother me.

FLANEUR Well...thanks for the smoke. *(FLANEUR EXITS. LIZZIE ENTERS, carrying a coat.)*

LIZZIE Herman...

MELVILLE What are you doing out here all by yourself?

LIZZIE You forgot your coat.

MELVILLE I don't need a coat. *(LIZZIE places coat on bench. MELVILLE, who is obviously quite cold, turns away.)*

LIZZIE You're going to get frost-bitten.

MELVILLE I'm *not* cold.

LIZZIE It's freezing.

MELVILLE But to make you happy, I'll...I'll put on the coat. (*He puts the coat on.)*

LIZZIE I brought you some gloves. (*MELVILLE puts on the gloves.)* Come on.

MELVILLE I don't see how you could ever put up with me... The never-ending writing, the reading...

LIZZIE I'm going to help you. *(JAMESON, whistling "Dixie," strolls by, upstage. EXITS in direction of FLANEUR.)*

MELVILLE Ever since the daguerreotype people expect a book to be like a photograph. Cheap entertainment.

LIZZIE Let's go back to the house.

MELVILLE But I'm going to give the reader as much fiction as my imagination permits. And reality. Truth. And poetry. And science, paganism—

LIZZIE We can talk when we get home—

MELVILLE And if the critics, or the public, or the goddamn termites don't like that, then to hell with 'em.

LIZZIE C'mon. (*LIZZIE takes HERMAN'S arm. HERMAN doesn't budge.)* It's freezing out here.

MELVILLE I need some more time.

LIZZIE I'm going back to the house. (*LIZZIE EXITS.)*

MELVILLE Lizzie. *(MELVILLE steps forward, reads, at times, from notebook.)* For all his tattooings, my new roommate was on the whole a clean, comely looking cannibal. But then the light was extinguished, and this wild cannibal, tomahawk between his teeth, sprang into bed with me. And giving a sudden grunt of astonishment, he... he began feeling me... Upon waking next morning just before daylight, I found both the cannibal's arms thrown over me in a most loving and affectionate manner. And as I opened my eyes he sprang from the mattress, switched off the light, and then hopped back under the blanket. (*BLACKOUT. MELVILLE laughs. Wedding-song music plays.*) You had almost thought I had been his wife.

Scene Three

(*A small cottage on Lake Winnipesaukee, New Hampshire, etc.*)

(*LIGHTS UP. Projection: THE COMPOSITION OF REDBURN.*)

LIZZIE This is such a perfect setting for a honeymoon. A cozy white cottage on a vast, placid lake.

MELVILLE Lake Winnipesaukee's just a puddle.

LIZZIE Well, it's not the ocean, but—

MELVILLE I wish we were lying side-by-side right now, on a straw mat... (*MELVILLE closes his eyes.*) On a soft white beach of a remote island in the South Pacific... Slow waves lapping the shore.. The cool, salt air lolling through the lazily leaning palms...

LIZZIE Perhaps you can take me there someday.

MELVILLE Wild drumming, chanting... Hungry savages dancing around a flaming, human-size pot.

LIZZIE We can travel to one of the safer islands.

MELVILLE But the only way for us to get there would be to sign on as crew members of a whaler.

LIZZIE I suppose I could cook.

MELVILLE For five straight years? On a cramped ship with a score of grubby, unbathed sailors... Nothing on the horizon but water, sky...

LIZZIE Well, if you could do it, I don't see why I couldn't—

MELVILLE Women aren't allowed on whalers. They're bad luck.

LIZZIE That's just an old superstition.

MELVILLE Ask any captain in Nantucket.

LIZZIE Every whaler I've ever seen has had a carving of a woman nailed onto the bow.

MELVILLE Carvings can't talk.

LIZZIE I'm sure I'd be perfectly capable—

MELVILLE You can't ship on a whaler unless you're a man.

LIZZIE (*pause*) So I'll disguise myself...as a gentleman... Robert Shaw.

MELVILLE Then you'd have to sleep down below on a hammock. In a wretched cabin with ex-cons, cannibals...

LIZZIE Well, if you were the captain, I could stay in the captain's cabin.

MELVILLE The crew might talk.

LIZZIE For sleeping with your wife?

MELVILLE Yes, if she has a moustache and her name's Bob.

LIZZIE I'd love to go on a voyage with you, Herman.

MELVILLE I've been on enough voyages.

LIZZIE But *I've* never travelled anywhere.

MELVILLE We travelled to Lake Winnipesaukee.

LIZZIE I mean to somewhere exotic. With savages.

MELVILLE We'll visit Barnum's freak show when we get back to Manhattan. *(MELVILLE tries to get amorous; LIZZIE turns away.)*

LIZZIE *(pause)* What was it like being with Fayaway?

MELVILLE She... Well...she can't be compared to you, Lizzie.

LIZZIE She must have been so beautiful.

MELVILLE *You're* beautiful.

LIZZIE After frolicking in the lagoon with Fayaway for two months, I don't see how you could ever be satisfied with a plain and proper woman from Boston.

MELVILLE Lizzie, you're so much more cultured, intelligent...

LIZZIE But...

MELVILLE What?

LIZZIE Nothing.

MELVILLE No. What?

LIZZIE You...

MELVILLE *(pause)* What?

LIZZIE *(pause)* You've never even seen my body.

MELVILLE We just got married this morning, for Christ's sake. And I wouldn't have married you if I didn't love your body, your mind...

LIZZIE I want you to be sincere with me, Herman.

MELVILLE You make me ecstatic.

LIZZIE You've never even seen me.

MELVILLE It doesn't take all that much imagination...

LIZZIE But it just can't be the same as when—

MELVILLE Com'ere. *(MELVILLE embraces LIZZIE, kisses her. She pushes away.)*

LIZZIE I thought we were going to go for a stroll along the pier.

MELVILLE We can walk in the morning.

LIZZIE You promised we'd—

MELVILLE We'll go after breakfast.

LIZZIE But I don't see how, after all your experience—

MELVILLE It's not all that complicated. (*MELVILLE puts his hands on LIZZIE'S shoulders.)*

LIZZIE Let me go change into that nightgown.

MELVILLE No.

LIZZIE It's so much more comfortable.

MELVILLE But then you're going from one set of clothes to another.

LIZZIE Well, one has to wear clothes.

MELVILLE Why?

LIZZIE *(pause)* Well...I mean, it's only proper. (*MELVILLE unbuttons his shirt, begins undressing.)*

MELVILLE This is better than proper. Actually, it is proper. Covering everything up so that it never sees the sun is what's improper.

LIZZIE It's only a flannel nightgown.

MELVILLE You don't need a nightgown.

LIZZIE It's quite cold up here.

MELVILLE I'm going to keep you warm.

LIZZIE *(pause)* I can't believe that this cottage doesn't even have a boudoir.

MELVILLE Lizzie, you're my wife. There's no need to hide anything.

LIZZIE It's not that I'm hiding—

MELVILLE I'll take your clothes off for you.

LIZZIE Wait. *(pause)* Let me... Let me at least go close the light. *(LIZZIE turns off the light. BLACKOUT. MELVILLE starts jumping around in the dark, screeching and acting like a monkey.)* Herman... Herman... Stop it... Just stop it, will you? *(We hear a door slam as MELVILLE EXITS.)* I'm uncomfortable enough taking my clothes off...with a man in the room... *(pause)* Well, I suppose I'll have to get over that, won't I? *(pause)* I mean, it's not exactly as if you're a stranger. You're my husband, for Pete's sake. *(LIZZIE eventually finds the lantern, turns light back on.)* Herman? *(MELVILLE ENTERS in LIZZIE's nightgown. He mimicks her.)*

MELVILLE Elizabeth... (*LIZZIE turns and sees MELVILLE, laughs.)*

LIZZIE Aren't...aren't you going to undress me?

MELVILLE Perhaps it would be best if you went into the other room.

LIZZIE There isn't another room.

MELVILLE Oh, my...

LIZZIE Do you want me to undress you?

MELVILLE But then you'll see my body... Well, I suppose you'll see it regardless...eventually. But, being a lady, I'd prefer if you would put on a blindfold first.

LIZZIE Well...

MELVILLE It won't take but a few seconds. (*MELVILLE blindfolds LIZZIE, spins her a bit.*) There. Now you can disrobe me.

LIZZIE Where are you? (*LIZZIE searches about. MELVILLE grabs LIZZIE'S ass.*) Herman. (*MELVILLE kisses her, moves away.*)

MELVILLE (*MELVILLE now speaks in his normal voice.*)(*pause*) Do you want me?

LIZZIE Yes... I think so. (*LIZZIE giggles.*)

MELVILLE Are you sure? (*MELVILLE takes a long, over-ripe plantain from a bowl of fruit, peels it.*)

LIZZIE Shouldn't I be? I mean, you are my husband.

MELVILLE Well, I've always been a bit modest.

LIZZIE Where are you?

MELVILLE Would you like...all of me?

LIZZIE (*pause*) Yes. (*LIZZIE giggles.*)

MELVILLE Are you sure?

LIZZIE Herman, where are you?

MELVILLE Com'ere. (*MELVILLE kisses her.*) Put your hand on that.

LIZZIE What?

MELVILLE Down here.

LIZZIE Oh... (*MELVILLE places LIZZIE'S right hand on the plantain that he is holding between his legs. LIZZIE pulls her hand back. MELVILLE returns her hand to the plantain, which she touches for a few moments.*) Ohhh...oh my... (*LIZZIE giggles.*)

MELVILLE It *is* edible, you know.

LIZZIE I'm not one of your South Seas cannibal women.

MELVILLE Goes down nicely with a bit of milk.

LIZZIE I'd rather just...touch it.

MELVILLE Pull on it.

LIZZIE Is that what Fayaway used to do?

MELVILLE Fayaway's rough, savage hands are no match for yours, my love. With their soft skin...thin, delicate fingers... Go ahead, now. Pull on it...

LIZZIE Well...

MELVILLE Hard.

LIZZIE Oh, I don't want to hurt you.

MELVILLE Just give it a yank.

LIZZIE (*pause*) I can't.

MELVILLE Actually, your hands make me feel quite nice.

LIZZIE (*LIZZIE becomes a bit more aggressive.*) Really?

MELVILLE Yes... Very nice... Mmm... And I'll feel even better if...if you pull on it.

LIZZIE Like this? (*LIZZIE tugs the plantain gently.*)

MELVILLE No, harder. Grip it tight and just...yank it.

LIZZIE I...I don't want to hurt you.

MELVILLE You *can't* hurt me.

LIZZIE Well...

MELVILLE Just do it, Lizzie.

LIZZIE No.

MELVILLE It won't hurt.

LIZZIE Well...I don't know.

MELVILLE It's our first night together...as husband and wife.

LIZZIE Well, all right... (*LIZZIE puts her hand on the plantain.*)

MELVILLE Grip it tighter.

LIZZIE Is this okay? (*LIZZIE turns her head away.*)

MELVILLE Tighter... Now pull.

LIZZIE I can't.

MELVILLE Just pull it. (*LIZZIE squeezes and yanks the plantain hard, inadvertently smashing it in her hand while pulling it away from MELVILLE. MELVILLE feigns pain.*)

LIZZIE Herman...I... (*LIZZIE drops the smashed plantain.*) Ahhh! (*MELVILLE laughs, pulls off her blindfold. LIZZIE realizes what happened.*) You're such a jerk.

MELVILLE Well, at least you have some experience now. (*MELVILLE laughs.*)

LIZZIE Yes...for ripping off your penis. (*MELVILLE reaches out to LIZZIE; she turns away.*)

MELVILLE Lizzie...I was just trying to...to loosen you up a little.

LIZZIE Well, there's nothing funny about—

MELVILLE Just relax, will you... You're all tensed up... (*MELVILLE kisses her passionately. LIZZIE pulls away.*)

LIZZIE I have to go wash my hands. (*MELVILLE pulls her back.*)

MELVILLE Wait until breakfast.

(*BLACKOUT. MELVILLE goes to his desk, writes, an action he continues throughout much of the play. LIZZIE has her own desk, on another part of the stage, where she copies MELVILLE'S manuscripts throughout much of the play. LIGHTS UP on YOUNG MACKIE (Y. MACKIE). A closed-circuit video camera transmits a close-up of his face. Or, throughout Act I—until the act's final scene—consider having Y. MACKIE appear only on video, perhaps utilizing video technology which would make him appear to be a hologram floating in the middle of the stage.)*

Y. MACKIE We're full of ghosts and spirits... Graveyards full of buried dead that come to life before us, within us... All our dead sires are in us. That's their immortality. From sire to son... We go on multiplying corpses within ourselves... Resurrections.

Scene Four

(SHAW'S parlor, Boston.)

(LIZZIE is very pregnant.)

SHAW Herman needs to be more practical. *(SHAW holds a letter.)*

LIZZIE He's been working extremely hard, father.

SHAW Listen to this letter he sent me... *(SHAW reads letter.)* "Truth is ludicrous, the silliest thing under the sun. Try to make a living by Truth and you'll end up in the soup kitchen!" *Truth*? I thought he was a fiction writer...

LIZZIE He's up in his study working from morning till night—six, seven days a week.

SHAW But he's not making any money.

LIZZIE Well, we have the trust fund.

SHAW That's *your* trust fund. And it's merely a supplement... He should have kept writing travel narratives.

LIZZIE But then he'd have to travel more.

SHAW Good.

LIZZIE Herman wants to write literature that examines racism, imperialism...

SHAW That's fine if he wants to live all by himself, hunched over an old desk in some Godforsaken hovel.

LIZZIE Well, he feels very strongly about negroes being granted the same rights as—

SHAW A successful person does not rock the boat by proclaiming ideals that go against those of the majority.

LIZZIE Segregation isn't something that one can just sweep under the rug.

SHAW But there's nothing that an individual can do about it without the majority's consent.

LIZZIE Roberts certainly has a valid case about Boston's negro children getting the same education as—

SHAW Right now, all you should be thinking about is taking care of yourself. And my future grandson. *(SHAW pats his daughter's pregnant belly.)*

LIZZIE Or granddaughter.

SHAW It's a boy. I could tell by the way you're walking.

LIZZIE You'd walk funny too if you were eight months pregnant.

SHAW (*SHAW looks at watch.*) We better get down to the station. (*They put on their coats. SHAW picks up suitcase.)*

LIZZIE Herman's really excited.

SHAW I should hope so.

LIZZIE He's going to be a wonderful father.

SHAW He just has to stop moving farther and farther away from what made him popular in the first place.

LIZZIE If you ever saw all the effort that he puts into—

SHAW All Herman has to do is give the people what they want. Which isn't all that much. *(BLACKOUT. LIGHTS UP. MELVILLE continues writing. LIZZIE copies MELVILLE'S manuscript pages. Boston courtroom. Projection: THE CASE OF ROBERTS V. CITY OF BOSTON. LIGHTS UP on courtroom.)*

ACTOR Hear ye, hear ye. The Supreme Court of the State of Massachusetts will now come to order. The case of Roberts v. the City of Boston.

SHAW While all races are created equal, there remains a clear distinction between whites and blacks. This distinction is one which the Almighty has seen fit to establish, and it is founded deep in the physical, mental, and moral natures of the two races. Indeed, no legislation, no social customs, can efface the distinction between whites and negroes. Thus, the court finds that segregated education for negroes is not only legal and just, but is best adapted to promote the education of that class of our population. (*SHAW strikes gavel. LIGHTS FADE on courtroom.)*

Scene Five

(MELVILLE'S study.)

MELVILLE (*MELVILLE reads, imagines.)* Girlish laughter emanates from beyond the port side of the ship. Young women wearing wreaths of white flowers swim out to the vessel, smiling, as the crew waves and whistles. The ladies shimmy up the side of the ship... Half-naked couples, civilized and savage, embrace upon the teak deck. Up against the masts, rails. Karky, the tribal tattooist, introduces me to an olive beauty with dark wet hair... *(LIZZIE ENTERS. She has just gone into labor and is in terrible pain. She often makes sounds in response to the pain as MELVILLE talks.)*

LIZZIE Herman.

MELVILLE She caresses my bearded face with her hands...

LIZZIE Herman.

MELVILLE Kisses my lips.

LIZZIE I'm going into labor.

MELVILLE What?

LIZZIE I'm about to have the baby.

MELVILLE Did you summon the doctor?

LIZZIE Your sister just went to get him. Ohhh... *(The audience sees LIZZIE'S pain intensify. MELVILLE returns to writing.) (pause)* I'm about to have the baby... Ohhhhhh, God...

MELVILLE I'm sure the doctor will be here any minute now, Lizzie.

LIZZIE Ohhh...

MELVILLE Just try to relax.

LIZZIE I have to go lie down.

MELVILLE Go ahead.

LIZZIE Ohhh... *(pause)* Well, aren't you going to help me?

MELVILLE. You need my help?

LIZZIE You *are* my husband.

MELVILLE Okay...

LIZZIE Well...

MELVILLE Let me just finish this sentence. *(LIZZIE leaves MELVILLE'S study in intense pain as MELVILLE writes, reads. She moves to another part of the stage, where she is in the throes of labor. She tries the breathing technique taught to her by a nurse. Her verbal responses to her pain sometimes occur as MELVILLE writes and speaks.)* He knows himself, and all that's in him, who knows adversity.

LIZZIE Oh... Oh, my God...

MELVILLE To scale great heights...

LIZZIE Oh, Goddd...

MELVILLE We must come out of lowermost depths. The way to heaven's through hell.

LIZZIE God help me... Ahhh...

MELVILLE We need fiery baptisms in the fiercest flames of our own bosom.

LIZZIE Oh, oh... please... Ahhh... Ahhh...

MELVILLE We must feel our hearts hot—hissing.

LIZZIE Oh, my God...

MELVILLE And ere its fire's revealed, it must burn its way out of us, though it consume us and itself...

LIZZIE Oh, where's the doctor?

MELVILLE At white-heat brand thyself, and count the scars like war-worn veterans over campfires...

LIZZIE Herman!

MELVILLE And howl in sackcloth and in ashes.

LIZZIE Ahhhhhh...

MELVILLE Know, thou, that lives that live are turned out of a furrowed brow.

LIZZIE Oh, ohhhhhhhhhh... God help me.

MELVILLE Oh, there's a fierce cannibal delight... *(LIZZIE screams in pain.)*

LIZZIE Ohhh... Ahhh...

MELVILLE In the grief that shrieks to multiply itself.

LIZZIE Herman!!!

MELVILLE Take it easy, will you?

LIZZIE Ahhhhhh...

MELVILLE I"ll be right there. *(BLACKOUT.)*

JAMESON *(Carnival music is played on a hand organ. The audience sees images that the physiognomist once utilized to prove that the African is lower down on the evolutionary scale than the Western caucasian. MELVILLE writes at his desk.)* What is it? What is it? The formation of the head and face of our specimen combines both that of the native African and of the Ourang Outang. What is it? The upper part of the head, and the forehead in particular, instead of being four or five inches broad, as it should be, to resemble that of a human being, is less than two inches!

Scene Six

(The Melville home.)

(MELVILLE writes. LIZZIE is asleep at her desk with the baby).

SHAW *(SHAW has a white silk scarf draped over his arm.)* "What I feel most moved to write, that is banned—it will not pay. Yet altogether write the other way I cannot. So the product is a final hash, and all my books are botches." "Dollars damn me... Dollars damn me!" *(Projection: THE COMPOSITION OF WHITE-JACKET. MELVILLE carries manuscript pages over to LIZZIE'S desk.)* Why does he keep sending these damn letters, just to infuriate me? He's got a wife and child to support, for Christ's sake. *(SHAW crumples letter a bit.)* Boy! Boy! *(BOY ENTERS.)*

BOY Yes, mastuh.

MELVILLE Lizzie.

SHAW Throw this in the fireplace, will you?

BOY Yessir. *(BOY EXITS with letters, scarf.)* Give me back my damn scarf. *(BLACKOUT on SHAW scene.)*

MELVILLE *(MELVILLE walks up to her, shakes her gently.)* Lizzie...

LIZZIE *(Talking in her sleep, with tremendous fear.)* No...

MELVILLE	Lizzie.
LIZZIE	(*Still sleeping.*) No... No...
MELVILLE	Lizzie...
LIZZIE	*(LIZZIE, in the midst of a dream, reacts with horror and shock.)* Aaahhh!
MELVILLE	*(pause)* I need you to copy a chapter of the new book.
LIZZIE	(*Half asleep and a bit scared.*) Whaaa...
MELVILLE	Are you okay?
LIZZIE	There...there was this woman, a witch, across a field... Two rattlesnakes at my feet... One black, the other white...
MELVILLE	You were just dreaming...
LIZZIE	Then the witch...transformed into a dark-skinned man, in a long black overcoat...
MELVILLE	Look, I wanted to ask you—
LIZZIE	Wait... They...the two snakes...they slithered up my leg, and...and began crawling into me—
MELVILLE	I need some help.
LIZZIE	I was going to pull them out, but the witch told me that as long as I keep the snakes together...
MELVILLE	Look, look...
LIZZIE	They won't bite...
MELVILLE	I need you to copy a chapter for me.
LIZZIE	What...what, uh...what time is it?
MELVILLE	Almost two o'clock.
LIZZIE	I thought the book was finished.
MELVILLE	I just need the one chapter right now...
LIZZIE	Can't you just use what you have?
MELVILLE	No. There are scribbles and scratches all over the place.
LIZZIE	It's *your* handwriting.
MELVILLE	I know, but it's a mess. And I...I can't really make proper sense of it until I can look at some clean pages.
LIZZIE	I'll do it tomorrow.
MELVILLE	But I need it now.
LIZZIE	It's two o'clock in the morning.
MELVILLE	I have to send a copy of the chapter to Harpers tomorrow.
LIZZIE	Why are you doing this to me? I'm nursing the baby all hours of the day and—
MELVILLE	I have to get this in so I can go over to England.

LIZZIE You're definitely going now?

MELVILLE I want to hand-deliver the proofs. And after writing all these books, the baby...

LIZZIE You hardly ever see the baby.

MELVILLE That's the main reason I want to get the book finished.

LIZZIE But then you'll be leaving for England.

MELVILLE I'll be able to get away from my desk for a while... Clear my head. Get ready for the next one.

LIZZIE I'm not ready to have another baby.

MELVILLE The next book. And I'll be able to strike a better deal for English publication if I can go over there myself.

LIZZIE I thought that Harpers was giving you a five hundred dollar advance.

MELVILLE They are, but that's only for America. I can get double that for English rights.

LIZZIE But you'll have expenses that you'll have to—

MELVILLE Your father said he'd pay for my passage.

LIZZIE But then you're going to be gone for Mackie's first Christmas.

MELVILLE Not if I sell the book right away.

LIZZIE I thought you were going to take a break after *White-Jacket.*

MELVILLE That's one of the reasons I'm going to England.

LIZZIE And what are me and Mackie supposed to do?

MELVILLE I'm not going to be gone that long.

LIZZIE And when were you planning on leaving?

MELVILLE Well, first I have to finish the book.

LIZZIE I thought it *was* finished.

MELVILLE Well, I...

LIZZIE You're just changing the one chapter, right?

MELVILLE *(pause)* I'm revising most of the book.

LIZZIE I've spent over two months copying out that manuscript, which nobody in the world could read except me...

MELVILLE *(At "read.")* I'm not about to send it out with mistakes.

LIZZIE There *aren't* any mistakes. I've corrected them all.

MELVILLE Some...sometimes you don't realize something's not working right until it's had a—

LIZZIE Maybe you ought to improve your handwriting so you can do your own copying.

MELVILLE Lizzie, I'm sorry... I know it's a lot to ask. But this is my fifth novel in four years and—

LIZZIE We have a son now.

MELVILLE Look...I've been writing and writing till my arm's about to fall off because I want to make money. (*BABY cries.*) And I've been doing that for several years. Most everyday—

LIZZIE The baby's hungry again.

MELVILLE I just need you to finish the one chapter for now.

LIZZIE I'll do it after breakfast.

MELVILLE I need it *before* breakfast.

LIZZIE I don't know if I can...

MELVILLE Once I sell the English rights to *White-Jacket*, we'll be able to buy that farm up in Massachusetts.

LIZZIE I'm exhausted.

MELVILLE You'll be fine... *(MELVILLE hands her a pile of manuscript pages.)* Here. I'm going to make a lot more money by bringing this over to England... I'll be able to relax, get my thoughts together... Oh...and here's the preface. *(MELVILLE hands her a few more pages. LIZZIE copies at her desk. LIGHTS FADE. SPOTLIGHT on MELVILLE, who holds a suitcase while glancing at and reciting the following passage.)* With a philosophical flourish Cato throws himself upon his sword; I quietly take to the ship. *(MELVILLE EXITS. Carnival music plays as the audiences sees a sailing ship quickly traverse the Atlantic.)*

JAMESON You will notice, ladies and gentlemen, how the ears are set back about an inch too far for humanity, and about three fourths of an inch too high up. They should form a line with the ridge of the nose to be like that of a human being. As they are now placed they constitute the perfect head and skull of an Ourang Outang, while the lower part of the face is that of the native savage. Step right up, ladies and gentlemen, and observe America's latest scientific discovery. *(During the following exchange, LIZZIE is in Boston, reading a letter, and MELVILLE is in London, speaking words from his diary. The characters' words, here, should overlap a bit, in this scene as well as in other montage-type scenes. And the characters should directly address the audience.)*

MELVILLE After dinner the rain ceased and we were slowly forging along under close-reefed topsails—mainsail unfurled. I was walking the deck, when I perceived one of the steerage passengers looking over the side. I looked, too, and saw a man in the water, his head completely lifted above the waves—about twelve feet from the ship, right abreast the gangway.

LIZZIE (*LIZZIE reads MELVILLE'S letter.*) At seven a.m. the Doctor and I sallied out and walked over Hungerford Bridge

MELVILLE For an instant, I thought I was dreaming; for no one else seemed to see what I did. Next moment, I shouted "Man overboard!" and turned to go aft.

LIZZIE We strolled over to Horsemonger Lane.

MELVILLE The Captain ran forward, greatly confused. I dropped overboard the tackle-fall of the quarter-boat and swung the rope towards him.

LIZZIE And we went to see the end of Mr. and Mrs. Manning.

MELVILLE A crowd of sailors and passengers were clustering about the bulwarks.

LIZZIE We paid half a crown each to stand on the roof of an adjoining house.

MELVILLE After holding onto the rope about a quarter of a minute the man just let go of it.

LIZZIE An inimitable crowd in all the streets.

MELVILLE And he drifted astern.

LIZZIE Police by hundreds.

MELVILLE The man could have saved himself.

LIZZIE People cheering...

MELVILLE I was struck by the expression of his face in the water.

LIZZIE Men and women fainting.

MELVILLE It was merry.

LIZZIE The man and wife were hung side by side.

MELVILLE No boat was lowered, no sail was shortened

LIZZIE Still unreconciled to each other.

MELVILLE Hardly any noise was made.

LIZZIE What a change from the time they stood up to be married together.

MELVILLE It turned out he was crazy and had jumped overboard, and that he had tried to leap into the sea with his infant son in his arms...

LIZZIE The mob was brutish.

MELVILLE The man drowned like a bullock.

LIZZIE Bloodthirsty. (*LIZZIE picks up baby.*)

MELVILLE All in all a most wonderful, horrible, and unspeakable scene.

LIZZIE (*LIZZIE writes letter and reads. The writing may be seen on video.*) It's such a pleasure just sitting in the rocking chair with the baby, holding him cupped in my arm. Watching his little mouth suck...his tiny fingers groping my breast... Herman finally found an English publisher, and he'll be home by the end of January. And he's begun working on his sixth novel...something about a whale... Mackie and I have had the most wonderful Christmas up here in Boston... And I'm finally feeling close to him... There's less tension... But not for father. The abolitionists are holding demonstrations, demanding that he ignore the Fugitive Slave Law... (*Baby cries. She stops writing, reading.*) And my dreams have started again... Last night, I was lying on my back, on a cold marble slab...in a mortuary, with Mackie on my left arm. Corpses on either side of us. But I wasn't dead. (*BLACKOUT.*)

Scene Seven

(Courthouse, Boston.)

(SHAW is reading through a thick, old law book. LIZZIE ENTERS with lunch in a brown bag. SHAW looks up, startled. In the background, a passenger ship travels from London to New York.)

SHAW Who let you into the courthouse?

LIZZIE One of the soldiers recognized me as your daughter... (*She gives him a chicken, which he eventually eats.*)

SHAW You shouldn't be coming anywhere near here. Not with that mob out there.

LIZZIE They're not going to harm you.

SHAW Well, with all the police and soldiers, the iron chains wrapped around the building...you wouldn't think so.

LIZZIE Somebody handed me this pamphlet, with a cartoon of Judge Lemuel "Rebel-Lover" Shaw whipping a black man.

SHAW That's absolutely ludicrous.

LIZZIE But why did you even consider that Mr. Shadrach, who was living freely in Boston, should be sent back down South, where he could be maimed, strung up on a tree... (*LIZZIE inadvertently puts pamphlet on SHAW'S desk.*)

SHAW Lizzie, I've never been eager to send a runaway slave back to his owner, but there are federal laws...

LIZZIE Everyone's saying that Shadrach should never even have been arrested.

SHAW When slave hunters from Atlanta present documentation to the court proving that Shadrach is a slave, and the law says—

LIZZIE Slave? He used to wait on us at Cornhills Restaurant.

SHAW Well, according to the law, if someone claims a person's a slave, then the slave must be returned to his owner.

LIZZIE Maybe it's just as well that the Shadrach case turned out as it did.

SHAW You want your father to become the laughingstock of Boston?

LIZZIE No, of course not. But there's certainly no reason you should—

SHAW I still can't believe that those negroes had the gall to barge into my courtroom this morning, pin the Deputy Marshall up against the wall—and while the Marshall's yelling, "Shoot him! Shoot him!"—carry

Shadrach down the stairs and through the streets, surrounded by a cheering throng of negroes and abolitionists that looked like a black squall.

LIZZIE Shadrach would never have been able to escape if so many people weren't in disagreement with the Fugitive Act.

SHAW *Most* Americans believe in the rule of law, unlike those rabble-rousers out there who want to keep fanning the flames of hatred...

LIZZIE I just hope you're safe.

SHAW Of course I'm safe. (*SHAW eats.*) If the North and South could only learn to respect each other, and cooperate, peacefully, then *everyone* would be safe, and Mackie's generation would be the beneficiary.

LIZZIE We have to get back to New York to greet Herman.

SHAW Well, thanks for the lunch, dear.

LIZZIE (*LIZZIE hugs SHAW.*) Take care, father.

SHAW Be careful out there. They're turning the streets into a goddamn battleground.

LIZZIE I'll see you next month. (*LIZZIE EXITS.*)

SHAW Those damn abolitionists, so help me God, will *never* again make a mockery of my courtroom.

Scene Eight

(A sideshow.)

(Projection: NEW YORK CITY. Next to JAMESON'S sideshow booth is the booth of VIRGIL VOX, VENTRILOQUIST, where VIRGIL operates a DUMMY. A musician plays carnival music on a hand organ as JAMESON waves a pointer and gives a spiel. FREAK sits behind a curtain.)

JAMESON. Looks like a Monkey!
Acts like a Man!
Looks like a Monkey!
Acts like a Man!

FREAK I need that money you owe me.

JAMESON Step right up and see
Ethnology's newest find:
New York's latest wildman freak,
Direct from the savage Marquesas,
Of the surly South Seas.

FREAK You gotta pay me my ten dollars.

JAMESON I told you, I'm gonna pay you as soon as we have a decent day.
(MELVILLE ENTERS, carrying a suitcase. "The Freak Spiel Song.")
Step right up now, and take a peek,
At a wild savage straight from the South Seas,
Come watch the world's tamest cannibal freak,
Speak words like "thank you," "gesundheit," and "please."
Hear the savage's tales of working on a whaler,
Of native life and poisonous darts,
Of capturing an American sailor,
Of heathenish orgies with grass-skirted tarts.
(JAMESON unveils FREAK.)
So step right up now, ladies and gents,
As the savage Karky drinks a cup of tea,
Come see in person, for only two cents,
Tattooed Karky, from the book called *Typee.*
(JAMESON discreetly takes a quick nip of whiskey, puts it away.)

MELVILLE Karky... Karky...

DUMMY Come on over here and see a real act.

MELVILLE You *are* Karky, aren't you... From Nuku Heva? *(FREAK looks straight ahead, although he seems as if he wants to respond.)* How the hell did you end up in New York?

JAMESON The cannibal don't tell his story, sir, except at fifteen minutes before and fifteen minutes after the hour. *(JAMESON closes curtain on FREAK.)*

DUMMY That show stinks.

MELVILLE He's...he's an acquaintance of mine...I think...

JAMESON *(Laughs.)* Which pub you comin' from, mate?

DUMMY Don't waste your time with that toothless cannibal.

MELVILLE I'm Herman Melville.

JAMESON Who?

MELVILLE The author of *Typee.*

JAMESON Yeah, and I'm the king of England...

DUMMY Come witness the mysteries of ventriloquy, polyphony, misogyny...

MELVILLE I met this man—

DUMMY *(To MELVILLE.)* Hey, is that a moustache or did you swallow a dog up to the tail?

MELVILLE I met him after jumping a whaler in the South Seas.

JAMESON Oh, so you're a whalin' man, too...

MELVILLE Well, I was... But not for long after I was kidnapped by cannibals.

JAMESON Kidnapped, were you, in the South Seas?

MELVILLE Yes.

JAMESON You and about nine hundred other sailors.

MELVILLE I wrote about it in *Typee*. (*MELVILLE holds up a battered copy of* Typee.)

DUMMY Hey!

JAMESON Sailors been tellin' that same old tale since before I was born.

DUMMY Come see a real show.

JAMESON Your story sounds a lot like the stage show over at the American Museum.

MELVILLE This is much different.

JAMESON Him and that Scottish ventriloquist are makin' a killin'.

MELVILLE Why don't you take a look? (*MELVILLE hands book to JAMESON.*)

JAMESON I really don't need anymore junk in my closet... Step right up and take a peek—

MELVILLE Karky, is Fayaway here?

JAMESON (*JAMESON begins skimming* Typee.) Look, I'm tryin' to run a business here, mate.

MELVILLE But we've known each other since—

JAMESON And if you keep this nonsense up, I'm gonna get the police over here. (*MELVILLE steps back.*)

DUMMY C'mon see a decent show.

JAMESON (*To self.*) Nobody wants to pay anymore.

MELVILLE (*Loud whisper.*) Karky.

JAMESON Damn drunks.

DUMMY How 'bout learnin' the ancient art of ventriloquism?

MELVILLE Karky.

DUMMY Learn all the secrets.

JAMESON I gotta get me a job in a theater.

MELVILLE (*MELVILLE pulls back FREAK'S curtain.*) Karky, listen.

JAMESON (*Gesturing to "NO FEEDING OR TALKING TO CANNIBAL" sign.*) You know how to read, mate?

MELVILLE But we're friends from back when—

JAMESON He don't even understand what you're sayin'.

MELVILLE But back in Nuku Heva—

JAMESON Spectators ain't allowed to talk to the merchandise.

MELVILLE Perhaps if I pay you.

JAMESON Two cents. (*MELVILLE pays.)*

DUMMY Sucker!

VIRGIL All right, that's enough. (*VIRGIL begins to put DUMMY down.)*

DUMMY No, no... C'mon. Hey... (*VIRGIL puts DUMMY down, removes hand from controls.)*

MELVILLE Karky, the last time we—

JAMESON No one's allowed to talk to the cannibal.

MELVILLE But I just gave you two cents.

JAMESON That's for admission when the show starts.

MELVILLE So I'll talk to him then.

JAMESON Look, I can't run a proper program if the spectators are gonna be talkin'.

MELVILLE It's absolutely essential that I speak with him.

JAMESON You wanna buy him? Two hundred dollars.

MELVILLE I can't afford two hundred dollars.

JAMESON Give me a hundred, right now, and you can walk away with him.

MELVILLE I'm not giving you a hundred dollars.

JAMESON Then you're not talkin' to him. (*JAMESON gives his spiel.)*

Step right up now, and take a peek,

At a wild savage straight from the South Seas...

MELVILLE I'll just talk to him after the show.

JAMESON That'll cost you fifteen dollars.

MELVILLE I'll give you five.

JAMESON Forget it.

MELVILLE Seven.

JAMESON Ten dollars and that's it.

MELVILLE All right. *(MELVILLE takes money from pocket, hands it to JAMESON, who puts the money in a cigar box.)* Ten dollars.

JAMESON Now you can only talk to him after all the shows are over. For five minutes.

MELVILLE When do the shows end?

JAMESON Seven o'clock.

MELVILLE That's four hours away.

JAMESON Well, that's the only time you can talk to him, and that's the end of this discussion.

MELVILLE But you never said that I'd have to wait—

JAMESON Look, you ain't allowed to talk to the cannibal till after the final performance. (*JAMESON sits down, skims through Typee.) (pause)*

MELVILLE *(To FREAK.)* Why are you letting them do this to you? In New York, of all places. The most cannibal city on earth.

JAMESON I warned you, beer breath. (*JAMESON EXITS. MELVILLE pushes aside curtain.)*

MELVILLE Karky... Why are you sitting up there? Karky... It is you, right? Look, you can talk now, he's not here... Hey, you do forgive me, don' t you? I mean, it was either me or you... I'm so relieved you're alive. And I want to help you get out of this place... You...you can go back to your island, Nuku Heva... I'll get you signed on as a crew member on a whaler... Just jump ship in the South Seas.

FREAK (*FREAK speaks without looking at MELVILLE.)* You wrote *Typee*?

MELVILLE You're...you're one of the book's major characters.

FREAK Karky's a freak.

MELVILLE No, no you're not a freak. Well, now you are. I mean, that's what you're being advertised as. But you're certainly not a freak in my book... And there's no reason to lower yourself to be a freak show exhibit so that some swindler can make all kinds of money off you.

FREAK You make money off Karky.

MELVILLE Right now I want to help you get out of here.

FREAK Then why you don't pay?

MELVILLE I'm not about to give that shyster a hundred dollars.

FREAK *(pause)* You never paid Karky.

MELVILLE I didn't have any money back then. I'd just jumped ship.

FREAK You pay now?

MELVILLE Look, I want to help you get away from this place.

FREAK Pay him a hundred dollars. (*SPECTATOR ENTERS. FREAK turns away from MELVILLE.)*

MELVILLE Karky...

FREAK (*Looking straight ahead.)* Boola, boola. (*FREAK strikes a pose while holding his spear.)*

MELVILLE I'll get you on a ship.

FREAK (*Threateningly.)* Maga-bohda-dah.

MELVILLE Make sure you get back to your village.

FREAK Mala... Mala... "Thank you." "Gesundheit." "Please."

MELVILLE You don't have to keep putting on this damn act. (*JAMESON and COP ENTER.)*

JAMESON *(To COP.)* He hasn't stopped talkin' to him.

COP So you think the cannibal understands English?

MELVILLE He was just speaking English.

JAMESON Like a parrot speaks English.

MELVILLE This man is an acquaintance of mine, officer.

COP Okay...

MELVILLE From Nuku Heva, in the Marquesas. When I was being held prisoner there, by cannibals, he at first was quite—*(COP pushes MELVILLE's back.)*

COP C'mon, bud. *(COP takes out handcuffs.)*

JAMESON I told you, officer.

MELVILLE What are you doing?

COP You're being arrested for public drunkenness and disturbin' the peace.

MELVILLE I...I was only having a conversation.

COP With a cannibal?

JAMESON He could hardly stand up when he walked in here.

MELVILLE I haven't had a drink all day.

COP C'mon, sport.

MELVILLE Karky... Karky... *(FREAK continues to look straight ahead.)* Tell them about Nuku Heva...when you used to serve me breadfruit...

COP Let's go sleep it off, mate.

MELVILLE I'm *not* drunk.

JAMESON He's been carrying on with the goddamn cannibal for the past fifteen minutes. *(COP tries to push MELVILLE along.)*

MELVILLE Look, I can prove our friendship. *(Gesturing to FREAK.)* He's...he's a central character in my book.

COP Oh, so you're a writer now.

MELVILLE I'm the author of *Typee*. And this so-called exhibit, he's right out of my novel. *(Gestures to FREAK.)* Even he'll tell you that—

JAMESON The cannibal ain't from no book. He's real.

MELVILLE You were just advertising him as Karky from *Typee*.

JAMESON *(To COP.)* I advertise him as bein' from a popular novel just to, uh...draw people in here.

MELVILLE Bollocks.

JAMESON You couldn't write no bleedin' book.

COP Even if you could, everybody in America knows that there ain't nothin' in *Typee* that's real.

MELVILLE Karky... Tell 'em... Tell 'em you know me.

COP *(To MELVILLE.)* C'mon, mate.

MELVILLE Tell them.

JAMESON He still thinks the cannibal comprehends him.

MELVILLE Well, if he didn't understand English, he certainly wouldn't be able to tell his story at fifteen after and fifteen before the hour.

COP *(To JAMESON.)* The cannibal tells a story?

JAMESON Actually, I, uh... *(Looks around, sees ventriloquist's booth.)* I use ventriloquism for that.

(MELVILLE walks over to FREAK, talks to him.)

COP You're runnin' a cannibal exhibit *plus* you're a ventriloquist?

JAMESON Yeah.

COP How'd you learn to do that?

JAMESON Well, I, uh... I learned ventriloquism while I was bein' held captive...in the South Seas...by cannibals.

COP Seems like all you need are a few more tattoos and a bit of music and you could be performin' your own stage show over at Barnum's American Museum.

JAMESON *(Gesturing towards MELVILLE.)* Look, he's at it again.

COP *(COP grabs hold of MELVILLE'S arm from behind.)* Let's go for a little ride in the wagon, bud.

MELVILLE I'm Herman Melville.

FREAK Gooh-lah-mahley-ohh.

(MELVILLE breaks away from COP, runs, and the COP turns to pursue the alleged criminal. From behind, while all eyes are on MELVILLE EXITING, FREAK trips the COP with his spear. FREAK sits, puts spear down. COP gets up, looks at FREAK. MELVILLE has unwittingly left his suitcase behind.)

COP Who did that? *(FREAK stares straight ahead.)* I said, Who did that, you daft prat?

FREAK Boo-lah-gah. Lah-mah-lah-mah-lah.

COP Stupid-ass savage. *(COP blows whistle.)* I'm gonna get that bastard. *(COP EXITS in pursuit of MELVILLE.)*

FREAK You gonna pay me?

JAMESON Yeah, once you start attractin' some customers.

FREAK You haven't paid me in over a month.

JAMESON So sell some fuckin' tickets. *(JAMESON walks over to VIRGIL'S ventriloquism sideshow. FREAK, unseen by JAMESON, begins putting on regular-looking clothes which he takes from duffel bag.)* Hey, mate...

DUMMY What does *he* want?

VIRGIL Why don't you ask him?

DUMMY You ask him yourself.

JAMESON Seems a bit slow today.

DUMMY You seem slow everyday.

JAMESON Hey, uh... You still sellin' that booklet on the secrets of ventriloquy?

DUMMY Now he's tryin' to steal our act.

JAMESON I just, uh...I wanted to give it to my nephew...for his birthday. He, uh...he's interested in learning ventriloquy.

DUMMY Ventriloquism. *(VIRGIL puts DUMMY in box, gets ventriloquism booklet. DUMMY'S voice is muffled whenever box's lid is shut.)* Hey, watch it, will you? Take it easy.

VIRGIL Get in there.

DUMMY Ow.

VIRGIL And keep your mouth shut. *(VIRGIL closes box, gets booklet.)*

DUMMY *(Muffled voice.)* Let me out. I can't breathe.

VIRGIL *(VIRGIL opens box.)* I said be quiet.

DUMMY Then let me outa here. *(VIRGIL closes box.)* Help, I'm gonna suffocate.

VIRGIL *(To JAMESON.)* The booklet's fifteen cents.

JAMESON Fifteen cents?

VIRGIL Sir, my treatise on the ancient art of ventriloquism contains scores of never-divulged secrets. And with the new techniques I've developed you'll be able to master rudimentary ventriloquial skills within minutes. And I've only two books left, so if you'd like to buy one...

JAMESON I'll give you eight cents.

VIRGIL Ten.

JAMESON Eight cents. That's my final offer. *(FREAK quietly EXITS with the duffel bag, JAMESON'S cigar box.)*

VIRGIL Look, for ten cents I'll throw in an illustrated pamphlet, for free, which tells of the time I was kidnapped by cannibals in the South Seas, forcibly tattooed.

JAMESON *(JAMESON hands VIRGIL ten cents, receives booklet and pamphlet.)* Here...

VIRGIL Good luck to yah.

JAMESON *(pause)* Business has been a bit off lately...

DUMMY *(From inside box.)* It's always off for you 'cause you suck.

VIRGIL *(VIRGIL opens box.)* Hey, this man does not come here to be insulted.

DUMMY Then where does he usually go?

JAMESON Hey, do you by any chance know where I can find a good tattoo parlor?

VIRGIL Well, there's Tommo's Tattoos over on Broadway and Houston...

JAMESON I think I'm gonna call it quits till tomorrow.

DUMMY That's way too short.

VIRGIL Good day, sir. *(JAMESON walks back to his booth while reading the booklet on ventriloquism. VIRGIL removes DUMMY from box.)*

DUMMY Hey, where's the cannibal?

JAMESON Karky... Karky! Lazy bastard ran off on another break... *(JAMESON notices that cigar box is missing.)* Hey, he ran off with my fifteen dollars, the thievin' skate...

DUMMY Looks like you'll have to go work for a change, asshole. *(DUMMY laughs.)*

JAMESON *(To VIRGIL.)* Did you see him leave?

DUMMY You talkin' to me?

JAMESON No, him.

DUMMY He's talkin' to you.

VIRGIL Me?

DUMMY Yes.

VIRGIL I didn't see nothin'. But I'll tell you what...if it was a slave that escaped, why his owner'd be willin' to pay five hundred dollars to the person who captures him and brings him back.

JAMESON Five hundred?

VIRGIL At least. But I'll tell you what...since we've known each other for a while, I'll go out and capture the savage for you for...for four hundred.

JAMESON Forget it.

DUMMY Three-fifty.

VIRGIL I'll do it for three.

DUMMY Two-ninety-nine.

JAMESON When I get my hands on that black bastard, he's gonna be swingin' from a goddamn street pole.

(JAMESON EXITS.)

VIRGIL I'm takin' a break, bud.

DUMMY Then what the hell am I s'posed to do?

VIRGIL Just get in the damn box and shut up. *(VIRGIL places dummy back in box and puts out a sign – BACK IN TEN MINUTES – and then EXITS. LIGHTS FADE. Scene shifts to another street in Manhattan. LIGHTS UP on MELVILLE. "Dixie" may be played during MELVILLE'S following narrative.)*

MELVILLE As I run down a narrow, filthy street lined with prison-like factories, a feeble wail springs from the earth. But there's not a soul in sight. I hear the dismal sound again, a low, hopeless, endless wail of someone forever lost. Then the shrill scream of the policeman's whistle suddenly seems to draw nearer, and I advance to an opening which communicates downward with deep tiers of cellars beneath a crumbling old cotton mill; and there, some fifteen feet below the walk, crouching in nameless squalor, with her head bowed over, is the figure of what appears to be a negro woman... Her blue arms fold to her livid bosom two shrunken things like children that lean toward her, one on each side. At first, I know not whether they are alive or dead. They make no sign; don't move or stir; but from the vault comes that soul-sickening wail. I make a noise with my foot, which, in the silence, echoes far and near; but there is no response. Louder still; and then one of the children lifts its head, and casts upward a faint glance, then closes its eyes, and lies motionless. The woman, also, now gazes up and perceives me; but lets fall her eye again. Observing that her two hands press against her bosom, and that something seems hidden under the rags there, a thought crosses my mind which impells me to forcibly withdraw her hands for a moment...and I catch a glimpse of a meager little babe, the lower part of its body thrust into an old bonnet. Its face is almost white.

SHAW *(LIGHTS UP on SHAW, reading a letter and drinking cognac in Boston.)* "It is my earnest desire to write those sort of books which are said to 'fail'."

MELVILLE It must have been dead some hours.

SHAW He has a son now and still, all he does is write.

MELVILLE The others are dumb and next to dead with want.

SHAW And then he goes on a trip...to England, of all places—spending my daughter's trust-fund money...

MELVILLE How they had crawled into that den, I could not tell...

SHAW And he's telling me that he wants to write books that "fail"?

MELVILLE But there they had crawled to die... I feel an almost irresistible impulse to do them the last mercy...

SHAW Where does he expect his family to live, in the gutter? So that he can tell the "Truth"?

MELVILLE And I pick up a large cinder block, ready to put them out of their misery, but I'm deterred by thoughts of law.

SHAW Son of a bitch... *(SHAW drinks cognac.)*

MELVILLE For I well know that the law, which would let them perish of themselves without giving them one cup of water...

SHAW Boy.

MELVILLE Would spend a thousand pounds, if necessary...

SHAW Boy!

MELVILLE In convicting him who should so much as offer to relieve them from their miserable existence.... (*MELVILLE realizes he doesn't have his suitcase.*) I knew I forgot something. (*MELVILLE EXITS.*)

BOY (*BOY ENTERS at "them."*) Yes, sire.

SHAW (*SHAW holds out empty glass, which BOY takes.*) Get me another cognac.

BOY Yessir. (*BOY EXITS. BLACKOUT. LIGHTS UP. MELVILLE ENTERS, goes to retrieve suitcase, sees COP approaching. MELVILLE takes out and puts on disguise, covers suitcase with his coat. COP ENTERS. MELVILLE feigns an English accent.*)

COP Did you see a drunkard run by here? (*MELVILLE shrugs.*) About your height... No hat... (*MELVILLE shrugs shoulders.*) Well, if you see 'im, be careful. He's very dangerous... A bleedin' nut-case. (*MELVILLE speaks to the COP in a feigned English accent.*)

MELVILLE He's wearin' no hat, you say?

COP Not even a cap.

MELVILLE Does this chap have brown hair, blue eyes... About my height.

COP Exactly.

MELVILLE Drunk as a bloody skunk?

COP He's been by?

MELVILLE I seen a man looks like that runnin' along the pier.

COP Musta been him. (*FLANEUR ENTERS upstage, walks across back of stage, EXITS.*)

MELVILLE You shoulda seen the bugger go. Like he was runnin' from a fire.

COP How do you know he was drunk?

MELVILLE Well, he stopped and asked me if I could make a contribution to the Fund to Restore Cannibals to their Native Lands. (*JAMESON ENTERS with giant, human-sized net on a pole, walks in direction of FLANEUR. COP notices JAMESON.*) And he smelled like a bleedin' bar rag.

JAMESON Afternoon, officer. (*JAMESON EXITS.*)

COP Where'd the drunkard go off to?

MELVILLE Saw him headin' towards a ship.

COP When?

MELVILLE 'Bout ten minutes ago. A sheep ship.

COP A sheep ship?

MELVILLE A ship with sheep on it.

COP I want you to show it to me.

MELVILLE Can't show you the sheep ship.

COP There ain't never more than one or two sheep ships in the whole damn port.

MELVILLE Quite impossible.

COP What?

MELVILLE To show you where he went.

COP You better shape up.

MELVILLE But if I can't show you the sheep ship—

COP (*COP puts his arm around MELVILLE.*) C'mon, we're goin' for a short stroll along the shore.

MELVILLE I can't show you much—

COP (*COP shoves MELVILLE.*) You *gotta* show me.

MELVILLE Don't shove me.

COP Where's the ship?

MELVILLE It was behind a shop.

COP What shop?

MELVILLE A shoe shop.

COP Shropshire shoes?

MELVILLE A shop in a shack.

COP Which one?

MELVILLE I'm not sure.

COP Show me. (*COP tries to get MELVILLE to move.*)

MELVILLE But the ship shoved off.

COP The sheep ship shoved off?

MELVILLE (*Shouting.*) Yes!

COP Don't shout... You're sure the ship shoved off?

MELVILLE With the sheep.

COP The sheep ship.

MELVILLE Sure as a shot.

COP Shit... And the drunkard got onboard?

MELVILLE Barely. They'd just pulled the gangway, and he had to make a running jump. Nearly ended up in the Hudson.

COP You sure it was him?

MELVILLE Well, I know he was a mad-drunk cannibal lover... About my height..blue eyes... (*JAMESON ENTERS with giant net on a pole, eyes DUMMY'S box, opens it, looks in, begins to EXIT.*)

COP Bloody con-man... They're crawling all over Manhattan these days...

MELVILLE I also saw something that I think you ought to investigate...

COP — You didn't witness a crime? *(JAMESON—unseen by COP or MELVILLE—walks over to DUMMY'S box, snatches it, along with DUMMY, who's inside, and begins to walk away.)*

MELVILLE — Well, yes... I believe it *is* a crime... A few moments ago I heard a terrible scream...

DUMMY — *(Muffled voice.)* Help me! Help!

MELVILLE — You hear it? I heard that before, comin' from beneath that old, abandoned cotton mill over there. So I ventured down below... *(JAMESON EXITS.)*

COP — That's private property, mate.

MELVILLE — There's a negro woman starvin' to death down there.

COP — She oughta go get herself a job in a factory.

MELVILLE — She's in a factory.

COP — I mean one that's still operatin'.

MELVILLE — They wouldn't let her into a factory. Not with three children.

COP — She's gotta use her resources.

MELVILLE — She doesn't have anything.

COP — Well, she's got three kids, doesn't she? She can sell 'em to a chimney sweep. That way she'll get some money for food, the kids'll all have work, and New York City'll be a better place for it. God knows Manhattan's got enough smokestacks can do with a good scrubbin'.

MELVILLE — Officer, this family's plight seems a matter of life and death, and—

COP — *(COP looks at watch.)* Look, my shift just ended.

MELVILLE — But they might not last to the end of the—

COP — They're outside my precinct. *(COP begins to EXIT.)*

MELVILLE — Someone has got to do something about those poor people down there. I mean they—

COP — Just worry about yourself, mate.

MELVILLE — I guess I'll just have to go back in there.

COP — Look, I live right around the corner here, and if I ever catch you inside of that building, I'm pinchin' you for trespassin'. *(COP EXITS. MELVILLE EXITS.)*

Scene Nine

(MELVILLE'S home, Pittsfield.)

(MELVILLE, obviously in pain from working at his desk for over twelve hours a day, writes with intense focus. LIZZIE, who is quite pregnant, copies manuscript pages. Projection: NEARLY TWO YEARS LATER. THE NEW MELVILLE

RESIDENCE: ARROWHEAD FARM, PITTSFIELD, MASSACHUSETTS. Projection: THE COMPOSITION OF MOBY-DICK.)

LIZZIE I'm just about ready to deliver my third child, but it hasn't been an easy pregnancy... Ever since we moved to Pittsfield, Herman's been anchored at his desk from eight in the morning till well past midnight writing about a white whale... In bed, he's constantly tossing, turning...mumbling in his sleep. If I so much as touch him, he jumps. Kicks the blankets... He sleeps with clenched hands, nails digging into palms. And he carries that tension with him throughout the day, amid a clashing of frenzies whirling around in his blazing brain, till the very throbbing of his pulse becomes insufferable anguish... At times, when these throes of anxious torment heave up from his base, a chasm seems to open up in him, from which forked flames and lightning shoot up. Accursed fiends beckon him to leap down, join them in the fire. When this hell in himself roars from within, a wild cry is sometimes heard throughout the house. And with glaring eyes he bursts through the door of his study as if escaping a burning bed. *(LIZZIE returns to her writing.)*

Y. MACKIE *(LIGHTS UP on Y. MACKIE, who may also be seen on video.)* What about the white whale? *(LIZZIE continues copying MELVILLE'S manuscripts, as she does throughout most of the play. Eventually, MELVILLE ENTERS with PHOTOGRAPHER, who is carrying the equipment of his profession.)*

MELVILLE I think we can set up right over here.

PHOTOG. That's fine with me, pal. *(The PHOTOGRAPHER sets up his equipment.)*

MELVILLE Can I get you a drink?

PHOTOG. To tell you the truth, I could go for a whiskey. But I still have three more appointments this afternoon.

MELVILLE Well, one shot's not going to hurt... *(MELVILLE pours shot, gives it to PHOTOGRAPHER.)*

PHOTOG. You know, I really shouldn't...but if you insist... Cheers, pal. *(He empties his glass.)*

MELVILLE At least you have a machine to help move things along.

PHOTOG. A machine cannot create art by itself... Sit down, please. *(MELVILLE sits in front of camera.)*

MELVILLE Do you realize that an artist like Rembrandt would take weeks, perhaps months, to paint a portrait.

PHOTOG. This is gonna cost you four dollars.

MELVILLE The publisher's taking care of it.

PHOTOG. I gotta get paid before I shoot.

MELVILLE Harpers arranged the appointment, right? So I'm sure they won't have any problem footing the bill.

PHOTOG. You know, I'm very busy and I don't got time to be nickle-dimed here. *(PHOTOGRAPHER starts packing up his equipment.)*

MELVILLE Here...here... I'll just need a receipt. *(MELVILLE hands PHOTOGRAPHER four dollars. PHOTOGRAPHER scribbles receipt on a napkin, sets up camera.)*

PHOTOG. Why don't you sit down in the chair? *(MELVILLE sits.)*

MELVILLE Considering how long it takes an artist to perfect a portrait, it's amazing how a machine can copy somebody's image in a couple of minutes—

PHOTOG. Please hold still, will yuh.

MELVILLE But a photographer cannot compare himself to a painter... Look at the portraits from the Renaissance. You can actually see the brush-strokes. The way the hand moved as it added layer upon layer of color. Texture...

PHOTOG. You'll have to hold still there for one minute now, champ, until the camera records your image.

MELVILLE I can't move for one minute? All right, but if I—

PHOTOG. And that includes your mouth.

(MELVILLE holds a pose for the PHOTOGRAPHER, who stands under a black piece of cloth that drapes both him and the top of his camera. The camera flashes, MELVILLE freezes, and the audience sees the "photo" slowly developing in black and white. Unbeknownst to MELVILLE, the PHOTOGRAPHER starts packing up and MELVILLE suddenly stands, walks away from the chair, speaks towards the audience. As he does this, a montage of images may suddenly appear behind his developing "photographic" portrait.)

MELVILLE It used to be that in order for America to have light, men had to sail half-way across the globe for whale oil... But everything's ephemeral now. Electricity, locomotives... One no longer has to work hard to make things... But machines didn't build the pyramids of Egypt. Men did. Shakespeare, DaVinci, Myron of Athens created art with their hands... *(Unbeknownst to MELVILLE, PHOTOGRAPHER EXITS.)* But now everyone and his uncle's gone out and purchased a camera so he can peddle black-and-white portraits... *(Closed-circuit video image of LIZZIE'S hands as she writes.)* But I'd much rather fail in originality, with my hands...than succeed in imitation. Only with his hands can an artist create something that's powerful, lasting... *(At "powerful", MELVILLE turns and is surprised the PHOTOGRAPHER has left.)* For four bucks he could at least say good-bye. *(MELVILLE looks at watch, returns to desk to write.)* Thinks he's an artist... *(LIZZIE walks over to MELVILLE'S desk, massages his shoulders. She's carrying a copy of the Literary World.)*

LIZZIE Where's the photographer?

MELVILLE Well, I...I guess he's all done.

LIZZIE Did you ask him about the family photograph?

MELVILLE A machine is not going to take our family portrait.

LIZZIE There's nothing wrong with having a photograph—

MELVILLE Any portrait of my family is going to be painted.

LIZZIE Photographs make you look quite handsome.

MELVILLE How can a camera make somebody look handsome?

LIZZIE The same way a painting can—

MELVILLE It's just a dumb machine that copies whatever's placed in front of it.

LIZZIE And your books aren't made by machines?

MELVILLE No. *I* make my books. And once I'm finished, *then* they go to a machine.

LIZZIE And machines are dumb, aren't they? But it's okay for a person to work night and day copying what you're writing. But a machine that makes copies, that makes life easier for the person who would normally paint portraits, there's something wrong with that.

MELVILLE I have to get back to my writing.

LIZZIE You're coming down for dinner, right?

MELVILLE Yes, I...I just have to finish this chapter.

LIZZIE You know, you promised you'd spend some time away from your desk once we moved up here.

MELVILLE Well, I...I went to that outing...

LIZZIE With Hawthorne and Duyckinck.

MELVILLE What's wrong with that?

LIZZIE You have a family.

MELVILLE I know, and I'm going to make more time for everyone...once the novel's finished... But I just couldn't turn down an opportunity to spend time with Hawthorne.

LIZZIE Hawthorne hardly even knows you.

MELVILLE I...I can't explain it... But even though I just met him, just...just being in Hawthorne's presence...our friendship... It's...it's already having a tremendous effect on my writing.

LIZZIE Well, it might be nice if you did something with your wife for a change. Or your children. *(Without looking up from his desk, MELVILLE tries to feel LIZZIE'S pregnant belly as he writes.)*

MELVILLE How's the new baby? *(His hand inadvertently slips down to her left knee.)*

LIZZIE Fine, I think. *(LIZZIE slightly moves her left leg.)*

MELVILLE I just felt him kick.

LIZZIE What? *(She slightly moves her left leg again.)*

MELVILLE He just kicked again.

LIZZIE Your hand's on my knee. *(MELVILLE looks up from his writing.)*

MELVILLE Oh... *(MELVILLE laughs, feels her stomach again.)* You feel ready.

LIZZIE I'll have given birth twice before you even finish your book.

MELVILLE Just let me write, will you?

LIZZIE You got some mail.

MELVILLE I'll look at it later.

LIZZIE *(pause)* An "anonymous" author in the *Literary World* really goes overboard here praising Hawthorne.

MELVILLE Hawthorne deserves to be praised.

LIZZIE *(LIZZIE reads.)* "To what infinite heights of loving wonder and admiration I may yet be borne.... Already I feel that this Hawthorne has dropped his germinous seeds into me."

MELVILLE *(pause)* What's wrong with that?

LIZZIE "He expands and deepens down the more I contemplate him, and further and further shoots his strong New England roots into the hot soil of my Southern soul."

MELVILLE Hawthorne's a genius.

LIZZIE And I'm sure Hawthorne will appreciate it... But I don't know why you took your name off the article.

MELVILLE *(pause)* What makes you think I wrote it?

LIZZIE You gave it to me to copy. Remember? I thought you weren't going to send this out.

MELVILLE I...I must have mixed it up with some of the whale chapters...

LIZZIE You're so obsessed with the white whale, you don't even know what you're doing anymore. You certainly don't have time for your family...but somehow you can find time to praise Hawthorne for over ten pages...

MELVILLE The article didn't take me that long, and I—

LIZZIE Did Duyckinck pay you for it?

MELVILLE That's not the reason I wrote it.

LIZZIE We need to repair the barn.

MELVILLE I'll be receiving checks from the novel.

LIZZIE It's not even finished.

MELVILLE It's...it's just about—

LIZZIE It's going on two years now. Just end it.

MELVILLE We'll...we'll have enough money for the barn.

LIZZIE You don't even know how to take care of a farm.

MELVILLE I used to work on my uncle's farm every summer.

LIZZIE Yes, back when you were a child. Now, you barely ever step out the door.

MELVILLE Well, I'm not about to sit at a desk for the rest of my life... And now that we have our own farm, once I complete this novel, I won't have to write as much. So I'll have more time with you...and the children... *(LIZZIE EXITS. MELVILLE writes for a while. As he reads the following passage, he seems to become increasingly ecstatic.)* After having my hands in the whale's spermacetti for only a few minutes, my fingers felt like eels... As I sat there at ease on the deck after endless hours of laboring, I bathed my hands among those soft, gentle globules, forgetting all about work. In that inexpressible sperm, I washed my hands and my heart of it. While bathing in that bath, I felt divinely free from all ill-will, petulance, malice... Squeeze! squeeze! squeeze! all morning long. I squeezed that sperm till I myself almost melted into it. Till a strange sort of insanity came over me; and I found myself unwittingly squeezing my co-laborers' hands in it, mistaking their hands for the gentle globules. Such an abounding, affectionate, friendly, loving feeling did this avocation beget that at last I was continually squeezing their hands, looking up into their eyes sentimentally, as much as to say—Oh, my dear fellows, why should we longer cherish any social conventions or acerbities? Come, let us squeeze hands all around. *(LIZZIE ENTERS MELVILLE'S study with more mail. He does not see her at first.)* Nay, let us all squeeze ourselves into each other.

LIZZIE There's more mail... Something from Harper Brothers... *(MELVILLE takes the letter.)*

MELVILLE I just wrote to Harper Brothers last week... I...I wouldn't be surprised if there's a check in here. *(MELVILLE opens letter, reads it.)*

LIZZIE No check? *(MELVILLE shakes his head no.)* Are they going to be sending one? *(MELVILLE throws the letter down on his desk.)*

MELVILLE Shit.

LIZZIE *(LIZZIE picks the letter up, reads.)* You *owe* Harper Brothers six hundred and ninety-five dollars?

MELVILLE I...

LIZZIE For what?

MELVILLE They must have made a mistake.

LIZZIE They've published books of yours. They're supposed to be *sending* you money.

MELVILLE I ordered a few volumes from them. But not that—

LIZZIE The books on whaling, right? And philosophy...

MELVILLE I needed information on—

LIZZIE It's as if you're *paying* Harper Brothers to publish your whale book.

MELVILLE I don't owe them all that money. *(MELVILLE returns to writing.)*

LIZZIE *(pause)* You have another letter.

MELVILLE I'll look at it later. *(MELVILLE, suddenly in great pain, stands.)* Ahhh... Goddamn sciatica... *(MELVILLE tries to walk through the pain.)*

LIZZIE It's from Mechanics and Farmers Bank.

MELVILLE I said I'll look at it later. *(MELVILLE tries to write; he's distracted.)*

LIZZIE *(LIZZIE opens letter from bank, reads it.)* Tomorrow's the last day to make a payment on the mortgage.

MELVILLE *(pause)* I thought I just paid that.

LIZZIE It's due on the first of the month.

MELVILLE Okay.

LIZZIE At the latest. Or they are going to foreclose.

MELVILLE Okay.

LIZZIE Tomorrow's the first.

MELVILLE All right. *(MELVILLE looks at his watch, reacts to sudden pain.)*

LIZZIE *(pause)* So you're just going to keep writing?

MELVILLE Harpers expected the rest of these chapters three months ago.

LIZZIE You should have just left it as it was.

MELVILLE It wasn't complete.

LIZZIE It wasn't complete for who? You? They've already printed a hundred and nineteen chapters.

MELVILLE You just don't understand.

LIZZIE What?

MELVILLE How...how important this book's going to be. I'm...I'm finally hitting my stride.

LIZZIE All those chapters have already been printed... And they're just sitting in a warehouse because you have to keep adding more. And more.

MELVILLE The book's just about there.

LIZZIE Just finish it!

MELVILLE I...I need...just a couple more chapters.

LIZZIE You'd think you were writing the Bible, for heaven's sake. But the publisher cannot keep waiting. The bank cannot keep waiting. I can't keep waiting. Mackie can't. *(MELVILLE stands, puts on his jacket.)* He's getting older now and he needs a father who's—

MELVILLE I'm taking the next train to Boston.

LIZZIE Boston? What are you going to do, rob a bank?

MELVILLE Well, there's someone...

LIZZIE Who?

MELVILLE An old friend of mine.

LIZZIE And he's just going to give you money?

MELVILLE Well...yeah.

LIZZIE Why?

MELVILLE Well...

LIZZIE Why would anyone give you money?

MELVILLE Well...we'll have to pay interest.

LIZZIE We're already paying interest.

MELVILLE I'll pay him off as soon as the book's published.

LIZZIE Wouldn't it be easier if you just got a job?

MELVILLE Look, look...I'm in a flurry right now. It's...it's all coming together. Which is why I hate to be bothered by this crap... But I'm going to take care of it. *(Looks at watch.)* I'll...I'll see you later tonight. Or tomorrow. *(MELVILLE, still in great pain, gathers his papers together. MELVILLE begins to leave. Stops.)* Oh, uh...when you have time...

(He hands her a pile of unbound, handwritten pages, quickly packs his shoulder bag, EXITS in a flurry. LIZZIE walks to her desk, places the pile down. She picks up a pencil, takes a blank sheet of paper. Stares at it, at the pile of MELVILLE's pages. Stands, looks at the work in front of her, then grabs MELVILLE's manuscript and heaves the pages into the air. LIZZIE feels a terrible cramp, rubs stomach.)

LIZZIE Oh, oh... *(She has a back spasm.)* Owww... *(LIZZIE carefully sits, begins crying. Eventually, Y. MACKIE ENTERS—or he may appear only on video here.)*

Y. MACKIE Mom... Are you okay?

LIZZIE Yes, Mackie... I'm fine. *(LIZZIE tries to compose herself. Y. MACKIE puts his arm around LIZZIE.)*

Y. MACKIE Where's Papa?

LIZZIE He...he had to go somewhere.

Y. MACKIE I want to show him the bird nest I found in the birch tree.

LIZZIE You can show him tomorrow. *(LIZZIE begins picking up the manuscript pages.)*

Y. MACKIE Tomorrow?

LIZZIE Help me pick these up? *(LIZZIE and Y. MACKIE methodically pick up the pages. Eventually, LIGHTS FADE.)*

ACT II

Scene Ten

(A stage show.)

*(JAMESON'S stage show could be performed away from the main performance area while simultaneously being transmitted, at times, on video. LIZZIE copies, MELVILLE writes. "The Sailor Meets the Savage Song." *Each line after an asterisk is sung only by the SAVAGE, who is played by the DUMMY, a dark-skinned ventriloquial figure. The DUMMY has been made-up to resemble JAMESON'S idea of what a cannibal looks like.)*

JAMESON (*and SAVAGE).

While working on a ship as a lowly sailor,
Hunting the sperm whale aboard a whaler,
We hit a wild squall, that tossed us to and fro,
But our captain kept drinking down below.
Despite the valiant crew, my efforts with the sails,
We were just beginning, the worst of our travails.
Lightning struck the spar, the ship began to list,
At the blink of an eye, all our lives were at risk.
I put out a small fire, the mast fell like an elm.
The third mate slipped into the drink, I took over the helm.
With every ounce of strength, I steered around a reef,
Just missed a giant boulder, dropped anchor near a beach.
Despite the drunken captain, a near mutiny,
I repaired the mast with a tall coconut tree.
Then in search of water, I strayed inland, all alone,
Where I came upon a platter, heaped with human bone.
I slipped and I fell as I started to my right...
(JAMESON falls.)
And there I was greeted by a most horrific sight.
(SAVAGE appears to right of JAMESON, who feigns fright.)
A tattooed cannibal, with sharp teeth and a knife,
(Here and elsewhere, SAVAGE could sing bass.)
*Me was hungry for his flesh.
I was praying for my life.

*Me was hungry for fresh meat.
I turned whiter than a sheet.
(BLACKOUT.)

Scene Eleven

(The yard of the Melville home.)

(Y. MACKIE is outside whistling "Dixie" and MELVILLE ENTERS with large envelope and a ball, although Y. MACKIE doesn't see him until he speaks to him.)

MELVILLE Are you ready to have a pass?

Y. MACKIE It's still morning.

MELVILLE Well, that's the best time to play.

Y. MACKIE You always work in the morning.

MELVILLE Well, now that the book's finished...

Y. MACKIE The book about the whale? *(MELVILLE smiles, nods affirmatively.)* It's all done?

MELVILLE Well, the printer still has to set and collate the final sixteen chapters, the epilogue...

Y. MACKIE Then why'd you come out?

MELVILLE I want to play with my son.

Y. MACKIE I don't want to mess up your book...

MELVILLE The writing's finished, Mackie.

Y. MACKIE You still have those other chapters...

MELVILLE They're finished. *(Holds up envelope.)* I just have to send them off in the mail. And then the book's going to be published.

Y. MACKIE I've been writing a story, too.

MELVILLE Oh, yeah.

Y. MACKIE You wanna read it?

MELVILLE Sure.

Y. MACKIE Let me go get it.

MELVILLE I thought we were going to have a pass.

Y. MACKIE I've been working really hard on it...

MELVILLE I'm sure it's brilliant, but let's have a pass first.

Y. MACKIE My story's about a boy. And his father's the king. And a writer, the most famous writer in the whole world. And because all the people in the kingdom like his writing so much, he has to keep writing...and writing. And his wife, the queen, she's always writing too. To help the king finish. And then the boy starts writing all the time.

MELVILLE You have to make time to play with your friends, Mackie.

Y. MACKIE I want to play with my dad.

MELVILLE C'mon, let's have a pass.

Y. MACKIE *(pause)* I have to go finish my story.

(Y. MACKIE runs away, EXITS. MELVILLE returns to his desk, writes, coughs periodically. He has considerable back pain. BLACKOUT. LIGHTS UP. MELVILLE and Y. MACKIE write in different parts of the stage. Eventually, Y. MACKIE may fall asleep while writing. LIZZIE writes, gets up, walks towards MELVILLE'S desk with manuscript pages that she just copied. Microphones (here and elsewhere) may transmit the sounds of everyone's writing. LIZZIE stops, reads.)

LIZZIE At rows of blank-looking counters sat rows of blank-looking girls, with blank, white folders in their hands, blankly folding blank paper. In one corner stood a huge frame of ponderous iron, with a piston periodically rising and falling upon a heavy wooden block. Before it stood its tame minister, a girl, feeding the iron animal with half quires of rose-hued note-paper which, at every downward dab of the piston-like machine, received in the corner the impress of a wreath of roses. I looked from the rosy paper to the pallid cheek but said nothing. *(MELVILLE, who is suffering from back pain, writes for a while, reads aloud. He coughs periodically. LIZZIE eventually ENTERS, unseen at first, to return a copied story.)*

MELVILLE Bartleby did an extraordinary quantity of copying, gorging himself on my documents. He ran a day and night line copying by sunlight and candlelight. He should have been cheerfully industrious. But he wrote on silently, palely, mechanically.

LIZZIE Your writing's becoming so much different.

MELVILLE Well, I'm not going to keep writing about sailors.

LIZZIE So now you're writing about me.

MELVILLE I'm writing *fiction.*

LIZZIE About blank women, who lead blank lives in a blank place with blank sheets of paper... *(MELVILLE writes.)*

MELVILLE They work in a factory.

LIZZIE For a man.

MELVILLE That's just a story.

LIZZIE You told me yesterday that you were going to mow the lawn.

MELVILLE I just have to finish this...

LIZZIE What?

MELVILLE *(pause)* This chapter.

LIZZIE You're writing another novel?

MELVILLE I have it all plotted out this time. *(MELVILLE writes.)*

LIZZIE We have three children... A farm, which isn't producing anything... I have to buy groceries for five people, wood... But don't worry about helping, or making money...

MELVILLE Why do you think I published all those books, stories in magazines? For fun?

LIZZIE At least the magazines pay something.

MELVILLE I can hardly even see what I write lately. Pain shoots through my fingers whenever I grasp my pen... I can't sit too long at my desk now because of the kink in my back...

LIZZIE Well, you certainly didn't strain it from tending to the farm.

MELVILLE *Moby-Dick's* going to sell.

LIZZIE So it's different than your other books.

MELVILLE *(pause)* I've made money with novels before.

LIZZIE Yes, your first two. *Typee* and *Omoo*. Which you wrote right after you got back from working on ships for four years. When people were still interested in reading about the South Seas...

MELVILLE Well, *Moby-Dick*, it's...it's the most powerful thing I've ever written.

LIZZIE That's wonderful...but if it's not a bestseller, you're going to have to find something else to do besides write... Like...like lecturing.

MELVILLE Maybe I should just put on one of those fur suits, advertise myself as the Missing Link... Barnum can feature me in his freak show: "Typee, the man who lived among the cannibals." *(MELVILLE has a coughing fit.)*

LIZZIE You can't just keep sitting at your desk writing for fourteen hours a day... Look what it's doing to your health.

MELVILLE Travelling through the snow and rain on a train, on coaches, all over the goddamn country, isn't going to make my health any better.

LIZZIE It would be so much easier for you.

MELVILLE I'm *not* a lecturer.

LIZZIE Then what are you going to do, Herman? Remain up in your study for ten more years, writing another stack of books that no one will buy?

MELVILLE *Moby-Dick* is going to be popular.

LIZZIE I hope to God you're right.

MELVILLE But...to tell you the truth, writing *Moby-Dick*...it took an awful lot out of me... And I think I could be a lot more productive—around the house, as a writer—if I could somehow manage that trip abroad I was talking about.

LIZZIE It's not as if you're eighteen years old and can escape on a ship whenever life gets difficult on land.

MELVILLE I'm not "escaping" from anything.

LIZZIE Go tell that to your son, Mackie. He was crying for over an hour after lunch yesterday.

MELVILLE He's just over-sensitive.

LIZZIE He said, "Papa never talks to me; he's always locked in his room." And the rest of the children feel the same way—

MELVILLE Maybe I should become more like Scribe...or Hugo. Hire a bunch of people to write formulaic books for me, and become a millionaire... Or I could hire out about ten guys with dark hair and beards to tell stories about living with cannibals...

LIZZIE So all you want to do is keep writing?

MELVILLE Just let me finish this novel.

LIZZIE No!

MELVILLE I have it all worked out—

LIZZIE You locked yourself away in your room for two-and-a-half years and you're *not* writing another novel right now.

MELVILLE Then let me take the trip to Egypt and the Holy Land.

LIZZIE I'm not asking my father for money.

MELVILLE The trip would give me a chance to...to get regenerated. And once *Moby-Dick* comes out, we'll be able to pay your father right back... And after being immersed in all the history over there, the art...I'll...I'll be able to produce all sorts of new material... And I swear, as soon as I return, I'll work around the house...every day... I'll even find a job if I have to...

LIZZIE Right now, Herman, all I want you to do is to mow the lawn.

MELVILLE Let me just jot something down first.

LIZZIE The grass is up to my waist!

MELVILLE I have to write a response to Rantaul's letter.

LIZZIE I thought you weren't going to get involved with the abolitionists...

MELVILLE I don't know.

LIZZIE If you're testifying for the side of the abolitionists...in father's courtroom, well...you could forget about your trip to Egypt.

MELVILLE If *Moby-Dick* pans out we're not going to need your father's money anymore.

LIZZIE The alleged slave hasn't even been charged.

MELVILLE But he's going to be.

LIZZIE Perhaps they won't need you to testify.

MELVILLE Rantaul told me that even if I can more or less verify that he's not a slave but a harpooner from the South Seas, your father is still going to find it difficult to rule against the so-called slave's "owner."

LIZZIE Then what do you think you're going to accomplish by testifying?

MELVILLE Well, that's what I have to sort out right now.

LIZZIE You can sort it out while you're mowing the lawn. *(LIZZIE EXITS. BLACKOUT.)*

Scene Twelve

(SHAW'S parlor.)

SHAW *(Projection: BOSTON. SHAW is drinking cognac. A double baby carriage and a stroller sit in the room.)* Last night, on Boston Common, in front of a thousand vigilantes, Wendell Phillips was out there maligning my name in terms that would hardly apply to a pickpocket. He even went as far as to counsel northern negroes to arm and defend themselves. That's treason!

Y. MACKIE *(Reading from Moby-Dick. Close-up of his face on closed-circuit video.)* What is it that in the Albino man so peculiarly repels and often shocks the eye, as that sometimes he is loathed by his own kith and kin!

SHAW These mad abolitionists are making Boston into a national joke...

Y. MACKIE It is that whiteness which invests him, a thing expressed by the name he bears.

SHAW *(To LIZZIE.)* What is he reading there?

LIZZIE *Moby-Dick.*

SHAW What's wrong with *Mother Goose*?

LIZZIE Keep quiet, Mackie. *(Y. MACKIE reads book silently.)*

SHAW Just the other day, Senator Clay—referring to this city's inability to return a runaway slave—stood up on the floor of the United States Senate and demanded to know whether Boston wanted a government of white men to yield to a government of blacks.

(The audience sees images—on video—similar to those from the scene in the film Birth of a Nation where men in blackface, several with their bare feet resting upon their desks, sit in the hallowed halls of Congress drinking, chattering, and eating watermelon.)

Y. MACKIE As if a dignified white man were anything but a white-washed negro...

SHAW I still don't understand why Herman had to make the whale white.

LIZZIE There *are* white whales.

SHAW Where? Where in the world can you point out even one white whale?

LIZZIE Well...for years sailors have been telling stories of a great-white sperm whale.

SHAW *Stories* of a white whale. I'll bet you that not one American sailor has ever actually seen a white whale. Yet Herman's whale is white, not black—like every other whale—but *white*, and it's a malicious killer, for one hundred and thirty-five chapters. And your husband has the gall to write such a book when racial tensions in America are at an all-time high. While my court's being forced to deal with the Fugitive Slave Law, slander from abolitionists like Rantaul and Dana...

LIZZIE Rantaul asked Herman to testify on behalf of Simpson.

SHAW Simpson hasn't even been arrrested yet.

LIZZIE Rantaul thinks that with his knowledge of the language and customs of the Marquesas, of whaling, Herman can demonstrate that Simpson is actually a South Seas harpooner who's always been free.

SHAW The last thing Herman needs right now is the abolitionists using him as a...a clown to turn my courtroom into a three-ring circus.

LIZZIE He's been talking about taking that trip to the Holy Land and Egypt again.

SHAW Well, tell him to go.

LIZZIE We can't afford it.

SHAW Well, then I'm going to send him a check.

LIZZIE That's too much, father.

SHAW Actually, I'll go right out this afternoon and book his passage. For next week.

LIZZIE I wish he'd just get a regular job.

SHAW He *can't* get a job.

Y. MACKIE Hey, grandpa.

LIZZIE Say excuse me.

SHAW Not until his condition improves.

Y. MACKIE Excuse me.

SHAW Maybe he'll be ready to work when he comes back.

Y. MACKIE Excuse me.

LIZZIE Mackie, your grandfather's trying to talk.

SHAW No, that's all right. What do you want, Mackie?

LIZZIE *(pause)* Mackie!

Y. MACKIE What?

LIZZIE Answer your grandfather.

Y. MACKIE What?

LIZZIE You said you wanted to say something.

Y. MACKIE Oh...

SHAW What's on your mind, son?

Y. MACKIE *(To LIZZIE.)* I wanna go home and see Papa.

LIZZIE Papa's going to be going out of town for a while.

SHAW On a sailing ship.

Y. MACKIE I wanna go with him.

SHAW While your father's away, Mackie, you, and your brother, and sisters—and your mother—are going to be able to take an extra-long trip to Boston. *(Y. MACKIE begins walking away.)* On Christmas day we can all go sledding—

LIZZIE Mackie, what are you doing? *(pause)* Your grandfather's trying to talk to you.

Y. MACKIE *(While glancing at Moby-Dick, he speaks as if possessed. Close-up of Y. MACKIE appears on video and/or a video hologram of Y. MACKIE may appear near the actor and speak the second sentence with him.)* I account it high time to get to sea as soon as I can. This is my substitute for pistol and ball. *(BLACKOUT.)*

Scene Thirteen

(Stage show.)

JAMESON Suddenly, a hundred spear-carrying tribesmen arose from behind the bushes. Fearing an imminent attack, I blasted my musket into the air and the savages began to bow. But I quickly ran out of gunpowder and the savages, their spears upraised, began closing in on me.

JAMESON (*and SAVAGE)

("The Close-Call with Cannibals Song." JAMESON sings. SAVAGE sings, solo, all lines preceded by an asterisk.)

Three savages dragged me towards the hell-like fire,

*The water it boiled, its steam was quite hot.

When they lifted me up, my fate it seemed dire...

*He soon would be dropped in a boiling pot.

I prayed to God, "Please forgive this sinner,"

*As we plopped him in a pot that was ever so big.

Then they banged on their drums as my skin began to simmer,

And I realized right then they might like the Irish jig.

So I sang an Irish song and they started to clap...

*And then we all howled, and we started to dance.

With the Celtic rhythm, they were all now enrapt.

And as they were dancing, I saw I had a chance.

So I leapt from the pot to the center of the ring,

*And as we were clapping he continued to sing...

And I laughed, and I jigged, and I sang, and I joked,

*Till all the pot's water had gone up in smoke.
The cannibals danced to my old Irish tunes...
*And we danced and we danced till the next day at noon.
And then they showed me their great gratitude...
*By takin' him away to have him tattooed.
And then they showed me their great gratitude...
*We took him away to have him tattooed.

Scene Fourteen

(Pittsfield train station.)

(MELVILLE carries a suitcase. FLANEUR wears white gloves.)

MELVILLE This is my substitute for pistol and ball. With a philosophical flourish Cato throws himself upon his sword; I quietly take to the ship. *(MELVILLE sees FLANEUR.)* Karky?

FLANEUR Pardon me?

MELVILLE Oh...you...you look like someone I know.

FLANEUR Leaving town?

MELVILLE I'm going on a trip. To Rome. And to Egypt, the Promised Land...

FLANEUR So you're not marching with the abolitionists today?

MELVILLE I don't have time to march with abolitionists.

FLANEUR So you're unconcerned with their cause.

MELVILLE No, I'm very concerned.

FLANEUR Then you ought to be out marching.

MELVILLE Excuse me. *(MELVILLE tries to move closer to train track.)* I have to catch the next train down to New York. *(FLANEUR blocks his path.)*

FLANEUR Some say that a slave is better off north of the Mason-Dixon Line. So I crossed the invisible line. And now, unlike before, I have difficulty securing food, shelter... Although negroes are allowed to read and write here, my children aren't permitted in the schools.

MELVILLE Things are going to improve, my friend.

FLANEUR Where?

MELVILLE Well, the North is certainly a place where negroes can attain some sort of freedom—

FLANEUR What are you doing to facilitate this improvement?

MELVILLE I... Plenty... I examine racism, slavery, oppression of the weak in the books that I write.

FLANEUR But when my children can't eat, of what use are your books?

MELVILLE Well...books can change the way people think.

FLANEUR And what if certain children aren't allowed to attend school with whites?

MELVILLE Look, my friend, nothing would please me more than to discuss these very pertinent questions with you, but right now I have a locomotive to catch. And then a Trans-Atlantic ship.

FLANEUR Have you marched with the abolitionists?

MELVILLE I do all of my speaking through my books, which, unlike street demonstrations, have permanence. Here, let me give you an example from one of my novels. *(MELVILLE reads the following line like a Shakespearean actor.)* "Let that master (the slave master) thrice shrive his soul; take every sacrament; on his bended knees give up the ghost; yet shall he die despairing; and live again, to die forever damned." For generations to come, such words can continue to enlighten.

FLANEUR Most negroes can't read.

MELVILLE But some can. And those are the people whose minds must first be changed. *(MELVILLE opens his suitcase, eventually takes out an enormous book.)*

FLANEUR *(Shows MELVILLE a flyer.)* Do you see this poster—"wanted for violation of Fugitive Slave Law, hundred dollar reward." That's a picture of me. But I've never been a slave.

MELVILLE Then you have nothing to worry about.

FLANEUR But the truth doesn't matter. Not if a white man testifies that I'm a slave.

MELVILLE I'm sure you'll be fine.

FLANEUR With all the posters about, I'm afraid I'll be arrested any day now. For no justifiable reason. But if you could testify, that I'm not a slave and that I'm actually from the Marquesas, I'll be able to remain free... If they send me down South I'll be enslaved, perhaps tortured and maimed... But if you could help me...with your testimony...

MELVILLE Look, I'd like to assist you. I really would, but I've had tickets for this trip for quite some time now, and it can't be postponed. And I don't even have any extra money to give you... But here... I'd like you to have a copy of my magnum opus, *Moby-Dick*. *(MELVILLE gives him book. FLANEUR sees JAMESON, hides face behind book. JAMESON ENTERS, carrying a large net.)*

JAMESON Hey, have you seen a black gentleman around these parts, about this tall?

MELVILLE Not lately, no.

JAMESON *(The following description can be altered a bit, to match the physical characteristics of the actor playing FLANEUR.)* Well...I want you to get in touch with me if you see one, 'bout thirty-five years old, five-foot ten... There's a hundred dollar reward in it for you.

MELVILLE Why, thank you, sir.

JAMESON *(To FLANEUR.)* How 'bout you... You seen anyone?

FLANEUR No.

JAMESON Could you...you do me a favor, sir, and, uh, distribute some of these wanted signs? Maybe you can even ask some of your neighbors to post 'em.

MELVILLE I'm afraid that such signs, if displayed around here, might encourage the wanted person to flee to a safer region.

JAMESON They ain't that bright... Here. *(JAMESON hands MELVILLE and FLANEUR wanted posters.) (To FLANEUR.)* And perhaps you can take a couple. *(FLANEUR, with face behind book, holds up hand, takes posters.)*

MELVILLE This man isn't a slave. He's not even African. He looks like a South Seas islander.

JAMESON They, uh...they change their appearance like that, in order to hide their true identity. But don't let him fool you. He's really a slave, Thomas Simpson, from down in Georgia. So make sure you contact me if you see him. And you'll be a hundred dollars richer for it... Oh...and in case you're gonna be in Boston next week, here's a half-price coupon for a top-a-the-line stage show...with ventriloquism, singin', a sailor escapin' from South Seas cannibals...

MELVILLE Oh, the drama's Shakespearean.

JAMESON Hibernian. And it's all true.

MELVILLE Thanks. *(JAMESON EXITS.)*

FLANEUR Thank you for *Moby-Dick*, sir. *(FLANEUR hands MELVILLE Moby-Dick, which is open to the beginning of the first chapter, and EXITS. MELVILLE glances in book.)*

MELVILLE I account it high time to get to sea as soon as I can... *(Y. MACKIE blows a train whistle.)* I quietly take to the ship. *(MELVILLE EXITS. The audience see images of pyramids, other symbols of the Middle East, of the Vatican, Rome, Jerusalem. Periodically, images depicting the violence of American slavery (and of contemporary American racism) and the wealth that slavery helped to create may appear, juxtaposed with images from the Holy Land. Appropriate music, sounds, accompany the images.)*

Scene Fifteen

ACTOR #1 *Moby-Dick; or The Whale*. Selected reviews.

ACTOR #2 It's God-awful.

ACTOR #1 An extraordinary book.

ACTOR #2 There's no method in his madness.

ACTOR #1 The general reader will throw it aside as so much trash.

ACTOR #2 Mr. Melville's Mad Captain is a monstrous bore.

ACTOR #1 A most extraordinary book.

ACTOR #2 Few books contain as much true philosophy and genuine poetry.

ACTOR #1 A perfect failure.

ACTOR #2 Mr. Melville has survived his reputation.

ACTOR #1 The work's inartistic.

ACTOR #2 He might have been famous.

ACTOR #1 Mr. Melville's ravings justify internment in a lunatic asylum.

ACTOR #2 The craziest fiction extant.

ACTOR #1 Utter trash.

ACTOR #2 A hundred times better had he dropped authorship with *Typee*.

ACTOR #1 The morals and religion of Mephistopheles.

ACTOR #2 Muddy, foul, and corrupt.

ACTOR #1 Herman Melville has gone "clean daft."

ACTOR #2 He's given us a very mad book.

ACTOR #1 Unnatural in concepton.

ACTOR #2 The author is mowing, gibbering, screaming, like an incurable Bedlamite, reckless of keeper or strait-waistcoat.

ACTOR #1 The style is maniacal.

ACTOR #2 Wholly unfitted for the task of writing. *(BLACKOUT on ACTORS.)*

Scene Sixteen

(The Melville home.)

Y. MACKIE *(Y. MACKIE is reading Moby-Dick, "live" and on video.)* The Albino is as well made as other men—has no substantive deformity—and yet this mere aspect of all-pervading whiteness makes him more strangely hideous than the ugliest abortion. *(Y. MACKIE thumbs through the pages. LIZZIE, in the midst of mending a sweater, ENTERS.)* This is my substitute for pistol and ball. With a philosophical flourish, Cato throws himself upon his sword.

LIZZIE Mackie!

Y. MACKIE What?

LIZZIE Why must you keep reading *Moby-Dick*?

Y. MACKIE I miss Papa.

LIZZIE He'll be home any day now.

Y. MACKIE You've been saying that for the past four months.

LIZZIE On such a long voyage, the...the ship often gets delayed.

Y. MACKIE Maybe it sank.

LIZZIE Trans-Atlantic passenger ships don't sink.

Y. MACKIE I'll betcha pirates boarded the ship in the middle of the Mediterranean... Killed everyone.

LIZZIE Your father's fine, Mackie.

Y. MACKIE Shouldn't we have heard something?

LIZZIE We're all going to go visit your grandfather for a while.

Y. MACKIE Again?

LIZZIE You ought to be thankful that he invites all of us to stay with him.

Y. MACKIE I wanna see Papa. *(Y. MACKIE plays with a toy gun. LIZZIE mends sweater.)*

LIZZIE You'll be seeing him soon enough. *(BLACKOUT. Split scene: Middle East/Pittsfield. Projection: MONTHS LATER.)*

MELVILLE "The Great Pyramid." *(Smoking a cigar, MELVILLE recites as a servant cools him with giant fan. A young girl, ELIZABETH, begins to cry off-stage. The crying gradually increases in volume.)*

Morn's vapor floats beneath your peak,

Kites skim your side with pinion weak.

(MELVILLE sips a cool drink from a coconut.)

LIZZIE Why is your sister constantly crying?

MELVILLE To sand-storms battering, blow on blow,

Raging to work your overthrow...

You—turn the cheek.

LIZZIE I'm...I'm sure there's a reason why your father's not home yet.

STANWIX *(off-stage). (Perhaps some of the action with the children is seen on video.)* Mama... Mama, Elizabeth's foot's stuck.

LIZZIE How did that happen?

STANWIX *(off-stage).* She, um...

ELIZ. *(off-stage).* Stanwix stuck it in the toilet.

STANWIX *(off-stage).* Liar! *(A loud thump and then baby cries.)*

LIZZIE Is your little sister all right?

ELIZ. *(off-stage).* I think she fell out of the crib.

LIZZIE What?!

ELIZ. *(off-stage). (A bit of water may fall from above.)* Owww... Stop flushing.

LIZZIE Stanwix!! *(LIZZIE EXITS.)*

MELVILLE Slant from your inmost lead the caves

And labyrinths rumored. Those who brave

And penetrate (old palmers said)

Come out afar on deserts dead
And, dying rave.

Scene Seventeen

(Shaw's parlor.)

	(SHAW is obviously quite ill and frail. He wears a robe, sits, perhaps, with a rubber hot water bottle on his head. He holds a wooden cane and often attempts to clear phlegm from his throat.)
LIZZIE	I think the house ought to remain in Herman's name.
SHAW	He's been gone for over seven months now.
LIZZIE	I'm sure he'll be arriving home soon.
SHAW	But he doesn't have any money to pay the note.
LIZZIE	*(pause)* I thought you were going to help us.
SHAW	I'm helping *you*. Anything you give to him, he just squanders. He told me he'd be away for four months, at the most, and that he'd publish a popular book based on his trip to Egypt—which is being financed by my money—and what is he doing? Writing poetry. Poetry of all things. While you're three months behind on the mortgage. So before he loses everything, I'm going to pay off the note, which will give me ownership of the property. And then I'm conveying the deed over to you. So even if Herman ends up going to debtor's prison upon his return...
LIZZIE	Father...
SHAW	Well, it could happen.
LIZZIE	We'll be fine once he gets a job somewhere.
SHAW	Your brother told me that Herman pushed you down the stairs while he was working on *Moby-Dick*.
LIZZIE	*(pause)* Where did he hear that?
SHAW	Mackie told him.
LIZZIE	Well... You know how clumsy I can be sometimes.
SHAW	Did Herman push you?
LIZZIE	Well...we were in the midst of an argument one night—because, well, I asked him for help with the children but he wouldn't stop writing—and I was at the top of the stairs, shouting, at the top of my lungs... So I can understand how Mackie might have perceived it that way... But no...I...as I was storming down the stairs, I merely missed a step...as I reared back to throw a boot at him. *(LIZZIE laughs embarassedly.)*
SHAW	So now you've resorted to throwing footwear.

LIZZIE I...I never thought I could act like that... But he just gets me so incredibly angry at times... And I...well... I talked to the minister... And he thinks that it would be best if the children and I...could get away...before Herman returns.

SHAW Then you'd be seen as an unfit mother for walking out on your husband.

LIZZIE By whom?

SHAW The state.

LIZZIE Well, Reverend Bellows seems to think I have valid justification.

SHAW But any judge is going to side with Herman.

LIZZIE Why?

SHAW Because you're a woman. So you'll be held responsible for making the marriage work. And if you insist on separation, you could very well be denied alimony because you'll be deserting your spouse. And even if by some remote chance the State of Massachussets would grant you a divorce, Herman would most likely countersue and be awarded all of the property, even the house that's in your name. He'll get the children...

LIZZIE You're just like every other judge.

SHAW I don't create the laws, Elizabeth.

LIZZIE *Somebody* must create the laws?

SHAW Why don't you just come to Boston more frequently. Enroll the children in school here.

LIZZIE Herman wouldn't agree to it.

SHAW He'd have less distractions... Maybe he'd finish his book of verse sooner.

LIZZIE *(pause)* I'll just go back home and try to be morally stronger.

SHAW At least the house is going to be in your name now.

LIZZIE But Herman's going to be living there.

SHAW Look, a friend of mine up in Lynn, Wyatt Evans, belongs to a Lyceum group that's been considering inviting Herman to speak.

LIZZIE Why would anyone pay to hear Herman?

SHAW He's a good storyteller.

LIZZIE Most of his books are out of print now.

SHAW But people still remember him from *Typee*, as "the man who lived among the cannibals." And I'm sure Herman would present himself well. And then that would lead to more speaking engagements, most of which would be out of town. So he'd be gone for weeks, perhaps months, at a time.

LIZZIE I wish he could start lecturing tomorrow.

SHAW I'll send a letter right off to Evans. *(SHAW chokes a bit, coughs.)*

LIZZIE Father...father are you all right?

SHAW Yes.

LIZZIE Let me get you some water.

SHAW I'm fine, Lizzie... It's just a...a bit drafty in here. *(SHAW coughs.)*

LIZZIE I wish you would just retire.

SHAW Not in the middle of the Simpson case.

LIZZIE Let someone else handle it.

SHAW If I don't see to it that the Fugitive Slave Law is enforced, then—

LIZZIE You don't need all this stress.

SHAW *(Coughs.)* I'm not going to retire until I see that you and the children, and this country, are back on track. *(SHAW coughs.)*

LIZZIE Let's go sit by the stove. *(LIZZIE and SHAW EXIT. BLACKOUT.)*

Scene Eighteen

(Shaw's court room, Boston.)

RANTAUL *(FLANEUR sits in chains.)* Your honor, I have here affidavits from Mr. Simpson showing that he was born not in Georgia, but in the Marquesa Islands of the South Seas. That he has been free for as long as he can remember, and that he never knew nor heard of his alleged "master," Mr. James Potter, until *after* his recent arrest.

SHAW That evidence is inadmissible.

RANTAUL Mr. Simpson is certainly as credible as the accuser. And he wears the tattoos of South Seas savages, speaks their language.

SHAW The law of 1850 clearly states that in no trial or hearing under this Act shall the testimony of the alleged fugitive be admitted as evidence.

RANTAUL Your honor, no slave residing in the North has ever been sent back to his owner under the Fugitive Slave Law. And we believe that our client's freedom is protected by the state's personal liberty law.

SHAW While the liberty law can apply to slaves, it does *not* apply to fugitives or runaways. And furthermore, the present circumstances do not warrant drawing the authority of the States and the United States Judiciary into conflict with each other.

RANTAUL But how else can a free man of color avoid slavery?

SHAW Mr. Rantaul, it is not within the jurisdiction of this court to examine such a question. We must merely observe the laws. And as to your earlier claim of unconstitutionality, during the drawing of the Constitution the document's framers, preferring to avoid the constant border wars that would result from hostile incursions across state lines to recapture escaped slaves, provided for state differences on slavery. And as a judge, I am here not to weigh in upon the morals of the Constitution, but to adhere to the wisdom of our forefathers who recognized the necessity of maintaining peace throughout the Union. Implementation of the Fugitive Slave Law—a Law passed by Congress and upheld by the Constitution—is an essential element in the formation of the Union, necessary to the peace, happiness, and prosperity of all the states. *(SHAW strikes gavel.)* The slave, Thomas Simpson, will be remanded to the agent who claims Mr. Simpson for his owner. *(COP handcuffs FLANEUR, hauls him away.)*

RANTAUL You're spitting in the face of the citizens of the United States.

SHAW I'm holding you in contempt of court.

RANTAUL You'll never get him out of Boston.

SHAW *(SHAW strikes gavel.)* I will personally make sure that Mr. Simpson is transported to his rightful owner, Mr. Potter of Georgia, even if the slave has to be accompanied by an army of five hundred. If we, in the North, knowingly set free a fugitive slave from the South, the foundations of our government will be irreparably shaken, and the American people—who have dwelt under the government's protection in unexampled peace and prosperity—will end up shedding fraternal blood in civil war. And as long as I am alive...*(SHAW coughs, strikes gavel.)* I will not allow that to happen. *(SHAW coughs uncontrollably. BLACKOUT. Music. The audience sees a sailing ship travel across the ocean. It arrives in New York. Y. MACKIE blows a train whistle. A train travels to Pittsfield.)*

Scene Nineteen

(The Melville home, Pittsfield.)

MELVILLE *(LIGHTS UP. MELVILLE stands next to his suitcase. LIZZIE has been taking clothes out of a basket and folding them.)* The statues were magnificent, Lizzie. Especially at the Vatican. I was standing this close to the Pieta.

LIZZIE Billy Cooper says it's too late to plant the turnips and potatoes.

MELVILLE *(pause)* So I can plant corn.

LIZZIE It's too late for that, too.

MELVILLE But I really benefited from the extra time abroad. The kink in my back, it's gone. My eyesight's improved. I haven't had sciatica since leaving—

LIZZIE You got a letter last week from First National Bank, the creditors for Dix & Edwards.

MELVILLE They've been sending you checks, right?

LIZZIE No, not checks... Bills. Dix & Edwards went bankrupt, and First National's collecting their outstanding debts. So now you *owe* money not only for your own short story collection, but also for *White-Jacket*.

MELVILLE But you've gotten some residuals...

LIZZIE No.

MELVILLE What about *Moby-Dick*?

LIZZIE You've received nothing but bills.

MELVILLE *(pause)* I'll get a job in New York.

LIZZIE We'd have to sell the house first.

MELVILLE That shouldn't be a problem, now that it's spring.

LIZZIE The roof needs patching. Paint's peeling off the shingles...

MELVILLE I'll start working on it next week.

LIZZIE You *never* work on the house.

MELVILLE But after being overseas for nearly a year, I...I'm completely rejuvenated.

LIZZIE You better start with the paint.

MELVILLE I will. As soon as I finish a couple of stories for *Putnam's Magazine*.

LIZZIE *Putnam's* went out of business.

MELVILLE They were publishing everything I sent them.

LIZZIE So was Dix & Edwards. But they've all gone bankrupt... Everything's going bankrupt. Banks, companies... But you did get a letter from *Atlantic Monthly*. They want you to write a new story. By June 15th.

MELVILLE I don't write on deadlines.

LIZZIE They're guaranteeing you fifty dollars.

MELVILLE I'm not about to let some upstart editor dictate when I'm going to finish a story. Do you think Michelangelo would ever work like—

LIZZIE Do you have any idea what's been going on back here? Father became the first northern judge to send a slave back down South.

MELVILLE Not Simpson.

LIZZIE Yes. And there are actually beggars now in Pittsfield. And Lenox. I don't think a week goes by without someone coming to the door and asking for a handout.

MELVILLE That's what sets America apart from Europe. This continual emphasis on money...

LIZZIE And how do you think we're going to eat, Herman? If you came home a month or two earlier, we could have had several crops planted by now.

MELVILLE But we're going to move to New York.

LIZZIE Nobody's going to buy the house until you fix it up.

MELVILLE I told you, I'm going to take care of it.

LIZZIE How are you going to pay for the paint?

MELVILLE Now that I'm feeling okay, I can bring in some more income from writing.

LIZZIE All your publishers have gone bankrupt.

MELVILLE There are other publishers interested in my—

LIZZIE Nobody wants to read literature.

MELVILLE Because they're not informed. But if all Americans could only walk into a place like Belvedere Chapel, and *feel* Apollo's presence, they...they'd be so mesmerized. And then that would inspire them to—

LIZZIE While you were gone mobs of angry men marched through the streets of Manhattan because they didn't know what else to do after losing their jobs... Abolitionists nearly rioted after father enforced the Fugitive Slave Law.

MELVILLE I had some fabulous conversations over there, and I'm convinced that if we could only get more people to value the aesthetic over the practical and scientific—

LIZZIE I have to go outside and take the clothes off the line.

MELVILLE Don't you want to hear about my trip?

LIZZIE Yes. But the kids need clean clothes for school tomorrow.

MELVILLE I'll take a walk outside with you.

LIZZIE Maybe you can fold some clothes. Help me put them away.

MELVILLE Sure... But I have to go upstairs first and write down some notes for a poem.

LIZZIE *Nothing* has changed, has it?

MELVILLE I have all sorts of ideas right now. About art, the Holy Land... The increasing racial tensions here at home. How it all fits together. Everything's suddenly very clear... And if I don't write it all down, right now, all of these images, these ideas...they're going to evaporate.

LIZZIE I need your help.

MELVILLE I'll be right back. *(Y. MACKIE ENTERS, stands in-between LIZZIE and MELVILLE. The violent tone of their argument quickly escalates.)*

Y. MACKIE Papa, wanna see my bicycle?

MELVILLE In a little while.

LIZZIE Your father's too busy.

MELVILLE I'll be right out, Mackie.

LIZZIE Your damn paper and ink are more real to you than your own family.

MELVILLE Well, if I can't generate material out of my travels, then the whole trip was just a waste of time.

LIZZIE *Life* is just a waste of time, isn't it?

MELVILLE At least some people respect me over in Europe.

LIZZIE That's because they don't have to live with you.

MELVILLE You can go to hell. *(MELVILLE goes to his desk, writes furiously.)*

LIZZIE C'mon, Mackie. *(LIZZIE begins to EXIT with a clothes basket in one hand and her other hand around Y. MACKIE'S shoulder. LIZZIE takes magazines and newspapers from basket, hands them to her husband..)* Oh...here are the reviews of *Moby-Dick. (BLACKOUT.)*

Scene Twenty

(Melville's study.)

(A caption reads: ELEVEN MONTHS LATER. LIGHTS UP, partly. MELVILLE, disheveled and drunk, is writing, drinking whiskey. CHARACTER ENTERS. MELVILLE sees him, drinks, tries to write. He reads his text.)

MELVILLE Strange, that in a work of amusement, a severe fidelity to real life should be demanded by anyone who, by taking up such a work, sufficiently shows that he is not unwilling to drop real life and turn, for a time, to something different. Yes, it is, indeed, strange that anyone should clamor for the thing he is weary of; that anyone, who, for any cause, finds real life dull, should yet demand that the author be true to that dullness. *(MELVILLE writes, drinks.)*

CHARAC. You've been home for almost a year now. The house is in shambles, your family's been starving for attention, and you've done nothing but write poetry and an incomprehensible novel.

MELVILLE Bollocks.

CHARAC. Oh... You've yelled at the children countless times, fought with your wife, let everything go to hell... So much for responsibility.

MELVILLE I have responsibility to myself.

CHARAC. And there's nothing else more pressing at the moment?

MELVILLE I...I address those things in my poems and novels.

CHARAC. What about life, Herman? When do you address that?

MELVILLE *(pause)* Every time I sit down at this desk.

CHARAC. At a desk?

MELVILLE Now why don't you just leave?

CHARAC. Because outside of this house, it's hunting ground for *men. Not* for thieves and robbers, but for men, like myself, who are guilty of no crime... *(MELVILLE laughs.)*

MELVILLE Why am I arguing with a product of the imagination? *(MELVILLE laughs.)* I have to stop doing this to myself... Begone shadow! *(MELVILLE laughs.)* Begone! *(CHARACTER remains. MELVILLE laughs, briefly writes.)* A fictional creature never existed, except in the powerful imagination which evoked him. And yet, a creature, a living creature, he is, though only a poet was his maker.

(CHARACTER laughs, wildly and without sound, as MELVILLE furiously moves his pen across paper, trying to write the CHARACTER away. CHARACTER remains in the study as MELVILLE drinks, writes.)

Scene Twenty-one

(Split scene: a Boston cemetery/MELVILLE'S study/the street.)

(A funeral song is played on a bagpipe. MELVILLE drinks, recites poetry.)

REVEREND We are gathered here in Boston on this fine April morning to celebrate the life of Chief Justice Lemuel Shaw, a just man who powerfully held to his convictions to the very end, continuing along the path of righteousness in spite of vociferous opposition from what was once a small but vocal minority.

HAWKER Extry!—a *Herald.*

REVEREND Lemuel Shaw maintained till the very end an enduring belief in the power of humankind...

MELVILLE *(MELVILLE is in his study, sober. He drinks a cup of tea, writes.)* So the winter died despairing...

REVEREND Of the country, to make the correct decisions, in the name of God.

MELVILLE And the weary weeks of Lent...

HAWKER Extry!—a *Herald.*

MELVILLE And the ice-bound rivers melted...

HAWKER Extry! Extry!

MELVILLE And the tomb of Faith was rent.

HAWKER Rebels bomb Fort Sumter. Civil War begins between North and South.

REVEREND Today, as Satan smiles upon Southern battlefields where brothers bloodily slay each other at an unprecedented rate, Chief Justice Shaw looks down from Heaven, shaking his head in dismay at how easily Lucifer has been able to lead innocent America to the slaughter. *(BLACKOUT on REVEREND and HAWKER.)*

MELVILLE O, the rising of the People,

Came with springing of the grass,

They rebounded from dejection

After Easter came to pass.

And the young were all elation.

Hearing Sumter's cannon roar.

And they thought how tame the Nation.

In the age that went before.

(Projection: THE COMPOSITION OF BATTLE PIECES, A BOOK OF VERSE. PITTSFIELD. LIZZIE ENTERS reading a letter. MELVILLE continues drinking.)

LIZZIE I received a letter from my father's attorney.

MELVILLE How much did he leave you?

LIZZIE Officially? Twenty thousand dollars.

MELVILLE That's wonderful.

LIZZIE But my father had given you several loans.

MELVILLE "Several"?

LIZZIE He paid for you to go overseas a couple of times...

MELVILLE He never called it a loan.

LIZZIE He paid off the mortgage...

MELVILLE So how much are we getting?

LIZZIE *(pause)* Nine hundred and fifty.

MELVILLE Less than a thousand dollars?

LIZZIE It's not as if he never gave you anything.

MELVILLE I know, but I, uh—

LIZZIE But what?

MELVILLE Nothing. I just thought it would pay some bills.

LIZZIE If it wasn't for my father, we wouldn't even be solvent.

MELVILLE We'll have to put the house up for sale.

LIZZIE The children love it here. Why don't you just get a job?

MELVILLE In Pittsfield?

LIZZIE Why can't you be like our neighbors, and plant corn?

MELVILLE I hate farming.

LIZZIE Then why did we ever move to a farm?

MELVILLE I'm sure I could get some sort of job in the shipping industry down in Manhattan.

LIZZIE In the midst of a Civil War?

MELVILLE New York's ports are busier than ever.

LIZZIE We *could* try to make the farm work. I mean, the kids could even help.

MELVILLE We *have* to move.

LIZZIE Oh...you've received a second letter from that person up in Lynn. They still want you to lecture.

MELVILLE Maybe I can do a monkey act. At the end of the lecture, I'll swing across the stage on a rope, toss coconuts out to the crowd.

LIZZIE Whether we move or not, if you don't start making some money, Herman, we're all going to be living out in the street. *(LIZZIE EXITS. BLACKOUT.)*

Scene Twenty-two

(MELVILLE's study / the yard.)

(MELVILLE drinks, writes a bit. The following lines should often overlap, although Y. MACKIE'S lines should be clearly heard. During the scene, we may hear (and see, at times, on video) a printing press, whose loudness may increase as the scene progresses. Y. MACKIE stands outside of his house with a copy of Moby-Dick, and addresses his words to the window of his father's second-floor study. On the video screen, we see MACKIE as MELVILLE sees him from the second storey.)

ACTOR #1 The critics on Herman Melville's *Pierre; or The Ambiguities*:

Y. MACKIE Papa.

ACTOR #2 His late works have been unsatisfactory.

ACTOR #1 Ridiculous.

Y. MACKIE Papa.

ACTOR #2 Corrupt.

Y. MACKIE Are you coming outside?

ACTOR #1 Melville's *Israel Potter*, selected reviews:

ACTOR #2 An oddity.

Y. MACKIE Did you start your next story, Papa?

ACTOR #1 A curt, manly, independent tone.

Y. MACKIE Do you wanna see my homework?

ACTOR #2 All of his late works are utter failures.

Y. MACKIE I wrote a new story.

ACTOR #1 The reviews of Melville's *The Confidence-Man*.

Y. MACKIE Do you wanna read it, Papa?

ACTOR #2 Melville's fancy is diseased; his morality vitiated.

Y. MACKIE Are you gonna come out?

ACTOR #1 A novel it is not.

Y. MACKIE Papa...

ACTOR #2 All his hard-earned fame may tumble...

Y. MACKIE Are you comin' out of your room today, Papa?

ACTOR #1 Nonsensical and ungrammatical.

ACTOR #2 The sooner this author is put in the ward the better.

Y. MACKIE I wrote a new story, Papa.

ACTOR #1 He totters on the edge of a precipice.

Y. MACKIE Just like you.

MELVILLE *(MELVILLE gets up from his desk, delivers the following line as if shouting down from the heavens.)* THOUGH I SHOULD WRITE THE GOSPELS IN THIS CENTURY, I SHOULD DIE IN THE GUTTER.

(MELVILLE pours whiskey into a glass, drinks, writes. The audience continues to see Y. MACKIE both "live" and on closed-circuit video. Y. MACKIE, who is holding a twig, puts his book down next to a tree and whistles, attempts to make bird-calls, in an effort to get the attention of his father.)

Y. MACKIE Papa!

MELVILLE *(Looking out the window.)* Hey, stop making a racket down there.

Y. MACKIE Papa, I got a can full of worms and I'm ready to go to the pond.

MELVILLE I'm in the middle of a poem.

Y. MACKIE You said you'd go fishin' with me.

MELVILLE I will... Later.

Y. MACKIE My friends' dads are always goin' fishin' with 'em.

MELVILLE Your friends' fathers aren't writing books... And if you don't stop pestering me, I'll never be finished. *(CLOSE-UP of Y. MACKIE'S distraught face on the video screen.)*

Y. MACKIE You promised.

MELVILLE Just leave me alone, damn it. *(Y. MACKIE, extremely upset, snaps the twig in front of his face as this image is projected on the video screen.)*

Scene Twenty-three

(Melville's study.)

MELVILLE *(MELVILLE, drunk, is still at his desk, drinking and writing.)*

So be cheery lads,

Let your hearts never fail,

While the bold harpooner...

(CHARACTER, whom MELVILLE has forgotten about, recites—from behind—the following line along with MELVILLE.)

Is striking the whale. *(MELVILLE glances at CHARACTER.)* No... You're...you're just something I made up...for a story... You can't talk. Stand next to me in a real room. *(MELVILLE laughs, tries to rid himself of what seems to be a bad dream. He eventually writes, reads.)* It may be that in his paper-and-ink investiture, the fictional creature acts more effectively upon mankind than would a flesh-and-blood one...

CHARAC. You really have to get away from your desk.

MELVILLE I don't know that anger against a man of straw is a whit less wise than anger against a man of flesh...

CHARAC. You can't keep going on like this.

MELVILLE Madness, to be mad with anything.

CHARAC. Stop what you're doing, Herman.

MELVILLE No.

CHARAC. Listen to me. *(CHARACTER picks up letter from MELVILLE'S desk.)* You must accept this lecture invitation.

MELVILLE I have to write.

CHARAC. You've done enough writing.

MELVILLE Cease shadow.

CHARAC. *(pause)* You have to stop. *(CHARACTER pulls MELVILLE up and out of his chair.)*

MELVILLE How did you do that?

CHARAC. You must abandon your desk, Herman. Things press too closely now.

MELVILLE *(MELVILLE begins to break down emotionally.)* I have to stay here and write. *(MELVILLE writes.)*

CHARAC. *(Forcefully.)* You can't write! *(BLACKOUT.)*

Scene Twenty-four

(MELVILLE home, Pittsfield.)

(Y. MACKIE, with intense concentration, is shooting a cap gun.)

LIZZIE Mackie... Mackie!

Y. MACKIE What?

LIZZIE Stop shooting the gun.

Y. MACKIE I have to practice.

LIZZIE For what? *(Y. MACKIE continues shooting.)*

Y. MACKIE I'm just practicin'.

LIZZIE What are you practicing for?

Y. MACKIE *(pause)* I wanna protect you.

LIZZIE *(Y. MACKIE shoots the gun.)* We're perfectly safe here. *(Y. MACKIE shakes his head no, shoots at some targets.)*

Y. MACKIE How come Papa stays locked up in his room all the time?

LIZZIE I want you to try to be really nice to your father, because you're not going to see him for a while.

Y. MACKIE Why?

LIZZIE He has to go work.

Y. MACKIE He works at his desk.

LIZZIE He's going to be doing a different type of work, now.

Y. MACKIE Papa's not going to write anymore?

LIZZIE He's going to be telling his stories in theaters.

Y. MACKIE I thought he *wrote* stories.

LIZZIE He's going to be telling stories from the stage now.

Y. MACKIE You think those kinda stories are more real than the ones in books?

LIZZIE Stories are make-believe, Mackie.

Y. MACKIE But what about when there's stuff in the story that's real?

LIZZIE Well, sometimes it's hard to tell what's real and what's not. *(Y. MACKIE shoots himself, feigns dying.)* Mackie, do not do that again or I'm going to take that gun away from you.

Y. MACKIE It's only make-believe.

Scene Twenty-five

(The lecture circuit, etc.)

MELVILLE Last night some kid was shooting spitballs at my face through a straw. No one tried to stop him. I still had twenty minutes to kill, but I skipped ahead to the last two pages anyway. And nobody even noticed. They were glad to get rid of me... Right now I'm in a tavern in Cleveland trying to decide between roast beef or trout... Waitress, get me another pint, will you? Hawthorne could have encouraged people to read my books... He could have helped me get that diplomatic post over in Italy... But he couldn't reciprocate. So now—as the war rages on down South—I'm performing in drafty, half-empty theaters, competing with blackface minstrels, exhibits of Philippine savages. Plays featuring human apes... I ought to be at my desk, writing. That's where I'm an artist. Not standing on some goddamn platform... When you're writing, it's just you and your thoughts. Alone. But when you're on stage and the audience doesn't like the performance, you...you feel such tension. Every moment you're up there. Night after night. And when the lecture's not going well, the tension increases. I clench the lectern, keep my eyes fixed upon my script...and begin to perspire. I look up, people are reading newspapers, leaving. A guy in the balcony's snoring... But in order to collect my pay I have to keep reading, for twenty more minutes.

Y. MACKIE *(Y. MACKIE reads letter; close-up on video.)* My Dear Mackie:

MELVILLE And my mind races back to sweat-filled nights in a ventless cabin on the *Acushnet*.

Y. MACKIE I hope this letter finds you and the rest of the family well.

MELVILLE To the mulatto whore in Milwaukee whom I wouldn't sleep with after giving her money.

Y. MACKIE And I hope that you have called to mind what I said to you about your behavior previous to my going away.

MELVILLE And then she laughed. Just sat there on my bed and laughed.

Y. MACKIE I hope that you have been obedient to your mother

MELVILLE As Lizzie and the children ate dinner a thousand miles away.

Y. MACKIE And helped her all you could, and saved her trouble.

MELVILLE Every town I go to now looks the same. Light comes with the flick of a switch. A steamship takes me back to the past.

Y. MACKIE Now is the time to show what you are... To show whether you are a good, honorable boy or a good-for-nothing one.

MELVILLE Nature's just a blur and nothing's as it was...

Y. MACKIE Any boy, of your age, who disobeys his mother, or worries her, or is disrespectful to her...

MELVILLE But I'm an entertainer now, not a philosopher.

Y. MACKIE Such a boy is a poor shabby fellow.

MELVILLE *(MELVILLE begins performing for lecture audience.)* Which reminds me of an incident during my recent voyage from Europe.

Y. MACKIE If you know any such boys, you ought to cut their acquaintance. *(Video images of "cannibals" and Y. MACKIE.)*

MELVILLE There was a tawny, tattooed man on-board rumored to be a cannibal...

Y. MACKIE Now, my dear Boy, good bye & God bless you... Your affectionate father...

MELVILLE And during our second night out the cannibal sat directly across from me at the dinner table. When it was time to take the tawny man's order, the waiter said to the savage, "Sir, would you care to look at a menu?" He said... *(JAMESON and SAVAGE ENTER.)* "No, but I wouldn't mind seeing the passenger list." *(MELVILLE laughs.)*

SAVAGE Ladies and gem'mens... We're proud to present to you 'da celebrated, tattooed Irishman in a true-to-life musical drama of his South Seas adventures... *(Music.)*

JAMESON Why, thank you, sir.

MELVILLE What are you doing? *(MELVILLE watches in disbelief.)*

JAMESON (*and SAVAGE) *("The Tattoo Song." JAMESON sings. SAVAGE sings, solo, all lines preceded by an asterisk.)*

After I's kidnapped by cannibals,

In the savage South Seas,

I escaped into the jungle,

And hid among the palm trees.
But I wasn't free for long,
From a fate I didn't choose,
The natives, they captured me,
And then they gave me tattoos.
For two long weeks,
I took thorns in the skin,
Tattoos from my feet,
Almost up to my chin.
The pain was so great,
I desired to yell,
But I grit my teeth,
And made it through hell.
Oh the natives were rude,
The maidens were crude...
*'Cause he showed no gratitude,
*For bein' tattooed.
Oh the natives were rude,
The maidens were crude...
*'Cause he showed no gratitude,
*For bein' tattooed.
(Music stops. Applause.)

JAMESON Good evenin', Mr. Cannibal.
SAVAGE Why, good ebnin' dere, sar.
MELVILLE What are you doing out here?
JAMESON The audience wants to see a *real* act...
MELVILLE I'm in the middle of my lecture.
SAVAGE They're gettin' tired.
MELVILLE But I've been contracted—
JAMESON It's time for the headliners.
MELVILLE Management never informed me—
SAVAGE The people want reality in their entertainment.
MELVILLE Reality?
JAMESON Here. A small gift. *(JAMESON hands MELVILLE a small jug of whiskey.)* Now be off...

SAVAGE You know what happened to da once famous author who swallowed two quarts of varnish?

JAMESON And what's that, sir?

SAVAGE Him had a fine finish. *(SAVAGE laughs.)*

MELVILLE Wait... You took Karky, from *Typee,* and made him into a freak exhibit.

SAVAGE *I'm* Karky.

JAMESON What's *Typee*?

MELVILLE My novel.

SAVAGE A novelty.

MELVILLE I gave you a copy.

JAMESON How could a real freak be from a fake book?

SAVAGE Don't try to steal me now for your story.

MELVILLE *Typee's* a novel based on things I've experienced.

SAVAGE And you know what's real, don't you? Don't you?

MELVILLE Of course I do.

SAVAGE Don't you feel stupid talkin' to a dummy?

MELVILLE Well—

SAVAGE Do you?

MELVILLE Well, yes...

SAVAGE Well, so do I. *(SAVAGE laughs.)*

JAMESON *(To audience.)* Now let's get on with the real show.

MELVILLE At least...at least let me paraphrase the rest of my lecture... *(Reads to audience.)* The statues of Rome, when compared to the plastic arts of the—

JAMESON You're a has-been. *(JAMESON walks towards MELVILLE.)*

MELVILLE They solidify the stature of—

JAMESON Get off the stage before I pummel ye with me fists, you limp fish.

SAVAGE Move it! *(JAMESON pushes MELVILLE, who falls over SAVAGE'S trunk. JAMESON and SAVAGE laugh wildly. MELVILLE stands, stumbles forward, with notes.)*

MELVILLE *(Disconcerted.)* The statues of Rome, when compared to the plastic arts of the United States, and to all the arts of the U.S... *(MELVILLE "gets the hook"; he's pulled off-stage as music plays. SAVAGE and JAMESON continue laughing.)* Hey...I...I have several more pages.

JAMESON I still think that gentleman deserves an opportunity to be on the stage.

SAVAGE Yes, he does. *(Shouting to MELVILLE, who is off-stage.)* And there's a stage leaving at ten o'clock... Get under it! *(SAVAGE and JAMESON laugh.)*

JAMESON After three months of forced tattooing I was carried aloft by Karky—the tribal tatooist who had become my dearest companion—and by three warriors to a gigantic banquet featuring breadfruit and roast canine. The chief's daughter, Fayaway, greeted me there and then, with assistance from Karky, she proceeded to tattoo a ring upon my left breast. At night, as the feasting continued, I learned that the chief's daughter's imprints upon my chest were part of a marriage ceremony, and that Fayaway was now my wife. My new bride, who was about fourteen years of age, was a most affectionate, faithful, and agreeable consort.

JAMESON (*and SAVAGE). *("The Canine-Breath Song.")*

Fayaway truly loved me,

*By land and by sea.

As I loved my savage bride,

*She gave him quite the ride.

Though there's one thing I don't miss,

*She ate dog-meat all the time.

And whenever we would kiss,

*It tasted like canine.

Though there's one thing I don't miss,

*She ate dog-meat all the time.

And whenever we would kiss,

*It tasted like canine.

(SAVAGE barks, laughs along with JAMESON.)

JAMESON Although betrothed to the chief's daughter, I was still a prisoner, under constant watch. One day, while out in the forest picking breadfruit, I felt something bump into my right side. It was Karky, who had suddenly appeared from behind an old coffin. I warmly greeted the cannibal, whom I had counted as a friend, but he merely stared back at me, with bulging eyes and a snarling mouth, as if ready to attack. I quickly reached for my weapon, only to realize that the savage had stolen it. *(SAVAGE holds knife.)* Give me back my knife.

SAVAGE Mine.

JAMESON Just give it back to me and I won't push the matter no further.

SAVAGE No... Mine now.

JAMESON *(To SAVAGE.)* Just give me the knife, mate.

SAVAGE I keep.

JAMESON *(Slowly.)* Give me the knife...now.

SAVAGE No.

JAMESON Give it to me.

SAVAGE Never.

JAMESON Okay... Com'ere... You see this?

(JAMESON holds up left fist, quickly covers SAVAGE'S mouth. They struggle as JAMESON attempts to put SAVAGE in coffin, which has a hinged lid (with hinges facing audience) not unlike that of a suitcase. Eventually, JAMESON puts SAVAGE – laying him on his back – in coffin.)

JAMESON You've had it, cannibal.

SAVAGE I ain't goin' in dere.

JAMESON Tryin' to steal my knife.

SAVAGE Get you hands offa me.

JAMESON You're gonna stay in the damn coffin until you rot. *(JAMESON finally puts SAVAGE in coffin. SAVAGE'S head rises up from coffin as they struggle.)*

SAVAGE Let me outa here, asshole.

JAMESON Asshole? *(JAMESON spanks him. SAVAGE makes sound of someone enjoying painful pleasure.)* You're close to an idiot.

SAVAGE Keep your mouth shut, nobody'll notice.

JAMESON I'm gonna give you the spankin' of your life. *(JAMESON spanks him.)* How does that feel?

SAVAGE That feel really good, sailor. Ohhh...you make me so hard. Just like Fayaway.

JAMESON You wanna see my belt?

SAVAGE You wanna see my woodpecker? It's gettin' longerrr...

JAMESON That's it.

SAVAGE Whatchu doin'?

JAMESON I'm gonna close the coffin.

SAVAGE I don't think you'll be able to. *(JAMESON closes lid. SAVAGE'S muffled voice is heard from inside coffin.)* Let me out. Let me out of here. Me can't breathe...

JAMESON *(JAMESON opens lid intermittently. Whenever coffin is closed, SAVAGE'S voice is muffled.)* Just shut up.

SAVAGE I give you one more chance to let me out.

JAMESON *(JAMESON places a large rock on coffin.)* Never. *(JAMESON walks away.)*

SAVAGE *(From inside coffin.)* You've had it, you hear me, sailor. You gonna get eaten. Eaten alive.

JAMESON I knew right then that I had to make my escape. *(JAMESON EXITS. BLACKOUT.)*

LINCOLN *(A profile of LINCOLN'S head appears behind a scrim and/or on video.)* This is essentially a People's contest. On the side of the Union, it is a struggle for maintaining in the world that form and substance of government whose leading object is to elevate the condition of men—to lift the artificial weights from all shoulders—to clear the paths of laudable pursuit for all—to afford all an unfettered start, and a fair chance, in the race of life.

Scene Twenty-six

(New York, etc.)

(Projection: New York City. Projection of images related to the Draft Riot on the streets of Manhattan. The audience also hears noise from the Draft Riot.)

JAMESON *(JAMESON reads letter, drinks from a bottle in a paper bag.)* Conscription? The hell with that... *(He continues reading.)*

HAWKER Read all about it! At the Battle of Fredricksburg, Meagher's New York Irish Brigade loses over 900 of its 1200 men! New York garment industry raking in record profits.

JAMESON They can stick their bloody draft up their arse. *(JAMESON burns draft notice, drinks. HAWKER sings "The Draft Lottery Song".)*

HAWKER We're coming President Lincoln,

Three hundred thousand more.

We leave our homes and firesides,

With our hearts bleeding and sore.

Since poverty has been our crime,

We bow to the decree.

We're the workin' poor who have no wealth,

To purchase liberty.

(HAWKER tries to sell papers.) Get your papers here, hot off the press. Meagher's New York Irish Brigade loses over 900 of its 1200 men at the Battle of Fredricksburg. *(HAWKER EXITS holding up newspaper.)*

COP Do you have your enlistment papers with you there, mate?

JAMESON Well...no. But I was just on my way home, officer.

COP You got your identification card?

JAMESON Umm...it's up in my apartment. But if you can give me five minutes...

COP C'mon.

JAMESON I, uh...I got some identification right here. *(JAMESON hands COP a poster advertising his act.)*

COP This is a freak show poster.

JAMESON See...see that guy in the big iron pot, next to the cannibal. That's me. And there's my name, Jameson.

COP Didn't you used to have a sideshow booth over on Fourteenth Street?

JAMESON Right.

COP *(COP begins to lead JAMESON away.)* Let's go down to the Union recruiting office.

JAMESON I'm an entertainer.

COP What's that got to do with conscription?

JAMESON Well, I'm gainfully employed, and—

COP Let's go get you measured for the Union blue.

JAMESON There's really no need for me to sign up, officer— *(MELVILLE ENTERS upstage, looks on as he walks, EXITS.)*

COP Then let me see your papers.

JAMESON I, uh...I'm hiring a substitute.

COP So you're in a position to hire someone to go fight for you?

JAMESON Yes, sir.

COP *(COP laughs.)* Except for that kettle you're standin' in here, I bet you ain't got a pot to piss in.

JAMESON I got the money to hire a substitute right here.

COP The hell you do.

JAMESON Three hundred dollars.

COP *(COP begins to lead JAMESON away.)* C'mon. You're gettin' measured for a blue uniform.

JAMESON It's...it's right here. *(JAMESON taps his pocket.)*

COP Three hundred dollars?

JAMESON Yeah.

COP Let me see it.

JAMESON Well...

COP Let's go, mate.

JAMESON Look. I got it right here. *(JAMESON pulls out a wad of cash.)*

COP Let me count it. *(COP counts money.)*

JAMESON You satisfied?

COP *(pause)* You stole this.

JAMESON I did nothin' of the sort.

COP You got your green card there?

JAMESON Well, I...it's—

COP	If you made this money without a green card, that means you received it illegally. Which means you stole it.
JAMESON	I earned that.
COP	Where?
JAMESON	Workin'. As a performer.
COP	Ain't no theater in New York gonna pay this kinda money for a cannibal stage show without a real cannibal.
JAMESON	I beg your pardon—
COP	You oughta be workin' with a big musket in your hands, marchin' through Alabama...
JAMESON	Gimme my money back.
COP	I'll tell you what... I don't like to see no one go hungry, and I know a man's gotta pay the rent... So, uh... I'll give you ten bucks.
JAMESON	That's my money, you thief.
COP	Actually...I'll give you five. *(COP gives JAMESON a five dollar bill.)* And if you keep actin' like a wise-ass, you're goin' to jail... *(LIZZIE ENTERS.)* And if I see your mug loiterin' around this neighborhood again, I'll make sure you go straight down to Richmond. That is, if they don't get a hold of your ass by then through the draft lottery.
JAMESON	That's my money.
COP	That's war money. Now get the hell outa here before I have you deported... *(COP pushes JAMESON; they EXIT. MELVILLE ENTERS.)*
LIZZIE	Herman. Where have you been?
MELVILLE	I...I was just out walking...and looking for work.
LIZZIE	Where's the bread?
MELVILLE	I, uh...Let me go get it.
LIZZIE	Your sister-in-law was preparing a big dinner. Remember? That's why you went out to buy bread.
MELVILLE	I'm sure there's a bakery right down the street.
LIZZIE	We already ate.
MELVILLE	Well...at least you all had dinner.
LIZZIE	Yes, after we waited for you until the food turned ice cold... The children were worried stiff.
MELVILLE	There was nothing to be concerned about—
LIZZIE	Didn't you see the smoke from those burning buildings?
MELVILLE	Well, yes, but—
LIZZIE	Mackie was afraid you'd been hurt.
MELVILLE	Well, if it's any consolation, I bought each of the children a book of poetry.

LIZZIE This is just such a wonderful idea, Herman, visiting your brother in the midst of a draft riot so that you can go job-hunting in Manhattan.

MELVILLE People are...they're just very emotional right now about the war.

LIZZIE Oh, is that why the Irish are throwing stones through storefront windows, pulling down telegraph wires, burning and looting banks....

MELVILLE They're also poor, and drunk. And they're no better off than the negroes, really. And they see other white men avoiding the draft by hiring working-class substitutes.

LIZZIE We'll be lucky to get out of New York before it burns to the ground.

MELVILLE No one's going to bother us at my brother's.

LIZZIE Yes. As long as they don't see his negro cleaning woman walk through the door...

MELVILLE There's never been a Civil War before. This race-related rioting...it's an anomaly.

LIZZIE So the young white woman ripping the pants off that negro corpse hanging by the neck from a lamp-post, and then slicing his testicles off with a steak knife... That's just an anomaly...

MELVILLE It's not fair to focus on the actions of one indvidual who's in the midst of a mob that's out of—

LIZZIE You want to live with these people?

MELVILLE I want to live in a city.

LIZZIE And what about our children?

MELVILLE Look, there will always be conflicts, rebellions. By Irish, negroes, abolitionists, rebels... Until we can put this damn slavery matter to rest. But as long as people care about the Civil War, passionately, for good or for ill, it's something that an artist has to examine, because right there, underneath even the most horrific symptoms, one can locate dramatic conflicts. Stories.

LIZZIE I thought we came to New York because you wanted to find a job.

MELVILLE Well, I secured an interview with the Customs office.

LIZZIE Let's just go back to Massachusetts.

MELVILLE I need to experience this.

LIZZIE Read about it in the paper.

MELVILLE But then I would only know it second-hand. So I couldn't really write about it. But if I can feel the heat of the burning tenements, the piercing shrieks of mad rioters, mobs ripping apart effigies of Lincoln, then I'll be able to *know* this unprecedented outpouring of human angst, bigotry...not only through words, but, most importantly, through the senses.

LIZZIE Why don't you just *stay* out here on the street.

MELVILLE But Lizzie—

LIZZIE Till next year for all I care. I'm going back to your brother's. *(LIZZIE begins walking away.)* And I'm taking the children home with me.

MELVILLE Lizzie, wait... *(LIZZIE EXITS. MELVILLE writes down notes. FLANEUR runs onto the stage. He is scared, breathing hard. The noise of rioting gradually increases in volume.)*

MELVILLE You really shouldn't be out here.

FLANEUR I just arrived in New York. Thinking I'd be safe once I reached the North.

MELVILLE Perhaps it's not so bad uptown.

FLANEUR Draft riots are breaking out all over the city.

MELVILLE There must be somewhere you could go...

FLANEUR Do you have a place?

MELVILLE I'm afraid my brother would be quite put out if I—

FLANEUR Where does your brother live?

MELVILLE Right on this block, but he—

FLANEUR I don't know where else to go.

MELVILLE If I had my own home here, I'd help you in a minute.

FLANEUR Perhaps you can at least ask your brother.

MELVILLE I'd feel very uncomfortable putting him on the spot like that—

FLANEUR I can't stay out here.

MELVILLE I wish I could help. But my wife and I are taking the train back to Pittsfield tonight. And there's really nowhere I could harbor you. But here...here's a dollar. Get yourself a room. *(MELVILLE EXITS. Noise from riot increases in volume. FLANEUR feels trapped, unsure of what to do next; he eventually EXITS. BLACKOUT. LIGHTS UP on stage show.)*

JAMESON *(To audience.)* As I ran down a barely marked path, I chanced upon a bamboo altar where I found, in a perfect state of preservation, three human heads. Their sunken cheeks were rendered yet more ghastly by the rows of glistening teeth which protruded from between the lips. Two of the three were heads of islanders; but the third, to my horror, was that of a white man. My imagination ran riot in these horrid speculations, and I wondered if Karky, my fair-weather friend, had planned on making me lose my temper in an attempt to convince the others that the tribe should add *my* head to their collection. I began running again and, upon reaching the peak of a hill, I was startled to see—off in the distance—a tall-masted schooner. *(JAMESON EXITS, as if towards schooner. SAVAGE arises from coffin.)*

SAVAGE *("The Eat 'Em All Up Song.")*

Da white man take our woman,

Him then made into chief.
Him give us naught but trouble,
Him nothin' but a t'ief.
Me talk to all de tribesmen,
To my plan, dem all say, "Yup."
We set a trap for da white man,
'Cause we wanna cook 'em up.
Eat 'em all up,
Eat 'em all up,
We gonna trap da white man.
And eat 'em all up.
Eat 'em all up,
Eat 'em all up,
We gonna trap da white man.
And eat 'em all up.
(BLACKOUT.)

Scene Twenty-seven

(Melville's parlor. New York City.)

(Projection: SEVERAL YEARS LATER... THE MELVILLES' NEW HOME. 104 E. 26TH ST., NEW YORK CITY. MACKIE is now close to eighteen years old.)

MACKIE But I'd like to finish school here.

MELVILLE That would be fine, Mackie, if you were a serious student.

LIZZIE It's not as if he did that badly.

MELVILLE Mackie can be educated as I was. Out in the world, working. If you really want to learn, Mackie, there's no need to listen to some pompous professor, who never penned an original thought in his life, tell you what a novel or a poem means.

MACKIE That's not the sort of—

MELVILLE Read the books yourself.

MACKIE I'm not interested in literature.

LIZZIE Mr. Lathers has offered you a very attractive position.

MELVILLE In a growing insurance company.

MACKIE As a clerk.

MELVILLE You'll be making over two hundred dollars a year. They'll serve you a nice, big lunch everyday. And if you perform well, which I'm certain you will, Mr. Lathers won't be the least bit hesitant to promote you. Which would mean more money, your own office.

MACKIE I could always find a job as a clerk. But if I don't finish school now—

MELVILLE You can study my philosophy and history books.

MACKIE You know...I've...I've always been interested in acting.

MELVILLE You can do that in your free time.

LIZZIE I'm sure there are plenty of amateur groups right here in New York.

MACKIE Why couldn't we just stay in Massachussets?

MELVILLE Don't raise your voice to your mother. *(MACKIE begins to EXIT.)*

LIZZIE Mackie...

MACKIE I'm going out.

MELVILLE Where?

MACKIE With some friends.

MELVILLE I don't want you hangin' out in those uptown joints all night.

MACKIE The job doesn't begin till next week.

MELVILLE Just make sure you're home by 10 p.m.

MACKIE Nobody in Manhattan even goes out until ten.

LIZZIE Your father's only thinking of your safety, Mackie.

MACKIE I'm going to be with a group of friends.

MELVILLE With all of the drinking, and whoring, and burlesque shows going on all night—and those Irish street gangs roaming around up there, looking for someone to take out their anger on—the Upper Eastside's like a powder keg sitting aside the sparks of a blazing furnace, just waiting to explode.

MACKIE You should have let me join the army.

LIZZIE You're much too young, Mackie.

MACKIE I'm almost eighteen.

MELVILLE This war's going to be over before you know it.

MACKIE Maybe I can still find work with a theater company.

MELVILLE You need a steady wage.

MACKIE But it's only insurance.

MELVILLE Great Western Marine Insurance is one of the biggest outfits in New York.

LIZZIE You'll have your own money.

MELVILLE You'll have job security.

LIZZIE And you'll be working just down the block from your father. You can walk to work together.

MELVILLE This is an excellent opportunity, son.

LIZZIE You'll be fine, Mackie.

MELVILLE I just hope you make the most of it.

MACKIE I'll see you later.

(MACKIE EXITS. Blackout. LIGHTS UP on HAWKER. "The Star Spangled Banner" plays in the background. On video: images suggesting the industrialization, prosperity, exploitation, and chaos that follow the Civil War.)

HAWKER Extry, extry! Get your *Herald* here! Get your *Herald*! *("The People's Victory Song.")*

After four years of war, no more civil tensions,

Lee gives up and the Union wins.

Our boys can come home, collect their pensions,

The South will atone for its darkest sins.

Northern profits at an all time high,

Less and less can the Northern worker buy.

From sacrifice, comes peace, for future ages,

Increased competition for lower wages.

Six-hundred thousand dead, a half a million maimed,

To save the black-man, and set him free.

Families destroyed, who are we to blame,

The cause of freedom, or the price of poverty?

Scene Twenty-eight

(Melville home. New York City.)

(Audience sees and hears images and sounds that suggest the increasingly busy city streets of New York. MELVILLE drinks tea, works on his poetry.)

MELVILLE To Sherman's shifting problem

No foeman knew the key;

But onward went the marching

Unpausing to the sea.

LIZZIE The Civil War's over.

MELVILLE Not for the hundreds of thousands who lost someone. Or for the people who fought in it. Or were affected by it. Which is virtually everyone. I mean, you can't even walk down Broadway nowadays without being accosted by a legless beggar with a Union cap on his head.

LIZZIE You really think people are going to want to read poetry about that?

MELVILLE Just listen to the title.

LIZZIE I've heard it a hundred times.

MELVILLE Listen to it. The way it sounds... *Battle-Pieces; Aspects of War. Battle-Pieces...*

LIZZIE It sounds like a board game.

MELVILLE Just the title alone is going to sell over a thousand copies.

LIZZIE So how were things at the Custom-House today?

MELVILLE I don't think I'll have to stay there much longer. (*Excited.*) These are the best poems I've ever written. Here, look at the proofs. *(MELVILLE offers the proofs to LIZZIE, who does not take them.)*

LIZZIE You haven't published a book in over ten years. *(MACKIE, wearing military-type uniform, ENTERS whistling "Dixie.")* People aren't going to remember you.

MELVILLE It doesn't matter.

LIZZIE It's certainly not going to hurt sales.

MELVILLE I just know this book's going to sell. It's got a great title. The poetics, they're innovative.

LIZZIE At least you have a steady job to go to.

MELVILLE There's not a more timely topic under the sun right now. *(LIZZIE begins to leave.)* Aren't you going to read the proofs?

LIZZIE I have to go take a roast out of the oven. *(LIZZIE EXITS.)*

MELVILLE *(MELVILLE, reads through proofs, moving his hand to the lyrics' rhythms. He seems pleased with his work. He does not look at his son at first.)*

There is a coal-black Angel

With a thick Afric lip.

MACKIE Dad...

MELVILLE And he dwells (like the hunted and harried)

In a swamp where the green frogs dip.

MACKIE Dad.

MELVILLE What, Mackie?

MACKIE I just, uh... I just joined a militia.

MELVILLE Hasn't anyone told you?

MACKIE What?

MELVILLE The war's ended.

MACKIE Well...you still need security.

MELVILLE That's why New York City has a police department. And I'm trying to read through my proofs right now.

MACKIE *(pause)* That's from your poetry book?

MELVILLE Yes.

MACKIE I, uh... I wanted to show you my uniform.

MELVILLE I'll look at it later.

MACKIE It's just like what the Union soldiers used to wear.

MELVILLE You're lucky you weren't old enough to be drafted.

MACKIE I probably would have enlisted.

MELVILLE Do you have any idea what it was like down there? Bodies and blood, everywhere. Men screaming their lungs out as their wounded limbs were being hacked off by a surgeon's rusty saw...

MACKIE I've read about it.

MELVILLE You can't understand the Civil War from reading... I was there. Near the front line.

MACKIE You never told me you were in the army

MELVILLE I, uh... I visited there for a couple of days...to gather material... For this volume of verse. But, of course, if they ever needed me...

MACKIE What were the battles like?

MELVILLE That's one of the things I try to capture in my new book.

MACKIE Can I see it?

MELVILLE You'll see it once the book's printed... I'll even give you a copy.

MACKIE Why poetry?

MELVILLE Because, well...the compact nature of poetry is best able to capture the intensity, the horrors of the Civil War. And I truly believe that this book contains some of my strongest writing.

MACKIE Stronger than *Typee*?

MELVILLE *Typee*? Stronger than *Moby-Dick*. This book's going to re-establish my name.

MACKIE I didn't realize that people read poetry anymore...

MELVILLE *(MELVILLE looks at MACKIE, notices he has a pistol.)* What's that?

MACKIE What?

MELVILLE In your pocket?

MACKIE Oh, uh... A pistol.

MELVILLE We're not living in the country anymore.

MACKIE I know, but I—

MELVILLE And I don't want any guns in this house.

MACKIE But I'm required to have one.

MELVILLE For what?

MACKIE The militia. Everyone has a gun.

MELVILLE Well, you're not going to keep a gun in the house.

MACKIE The only reason I have it is...is for protecting people.

MELVILLE Get it out of here.

MACKIE But if ever I get a call—

MELVILLE Just take it back to wherever you got it from.

MACKIE But if they find out I don't have a pistol, I'll get kicked out of the militia.

MELVILLE There are *no* guns allowed in this house. Period.

MACKIE *(Angrily.)* Fine.

MELVILLE There's enough violence out on the goddamn street... And you better not plan on staying out late tonight.

MACKIE I haven't been late for work once.

MELVILLE Well, I don't want you coming in late to this house anymore.

MACKIE What am I going to do here all night?

MELVILLE This is my house, and my rules...

MACKIE Yes, but—

MELVILLE And I don't want any back talk... Do you understand that? (*pause*) Do you?

MACKIE Yes, father. *(MACKIE EXITS and goes to his bedroom. MELVILLE continues reading his poem.)*

MELVILLE By night there is fear in the City,

Through darkness a star soareth on... Mackie!

MACKIE What?

MELVILLE I told you to get rid of the gun.

MACKIE I will...I'm leaving right now. *(MACKIE walks past MELVILLE, EXITS.)*

MELVILLE There's a scream that screams up to the zenith,

Then the poise of a meteor lone—

Lighting far the pale fright of faces,

And downward the coming is seen;

Then the rush, and the burst, and the havoc,

And wails and shrieks between.

(BLACKOUT. Stage show continues.)

JAMESON *(There is "primitive" drumming, which may continue until SCHOLAR appears.)* As I ran towards the ship, the furious beating of drums filled the woods. And as I neared the shore, running as fast as I possibly could, Karky suddenly appeared out of thin air, to tell me that the tribe was having a festival in my honor. He told me to wait, and went to get some men to carry me back to the village. As the drumming quickly intensified I sprinted towards the sea, reaching a clearing near shore where a boat from the ship, a whaler out of Nantucket, was just pulling away from the beach. I hollered out to the crew, explained that I was being pursued by cannibals, and the oarsmen agreed to take me back to the ship. So I ran out to greet them. *(JAMESON EXITS, as if going to greet boat. SAVAGE appears.)*

SAVAGE The warriors and me,
We arrive on the beach,
Surprised to see the white man,
Is almost out of reach.
So we have Fayaway cry out,
Tell him to return with haste.
'Cause he'll need some time to marinate,
So we can season him to taste.
(SAVAGE laughs.)

Scene Twenty-nine

(The Melville home, New York.)

ACTOR *Battle Pieces, and Aspects of the War*: the reviews: His poetry runs into the epileptic.

LIZZIE *(LIZZIE is reading review.)* His rhymes are fearful.

ACTOR Nature did not make him a poet.

LIZZIE *(MELVILLE, who has been drinking, ENTERS with briefcase as LIZZIE is reading review.)* It reminds you not only of no poetry you have ever read, but of no life you have ever known. Has there really been a great war, with battles fought by men and bewailed by women. Or is it only that Mr. Melville's consciousness has been perturbed, and filled with the phantasms of enlistments, marches, fights in the air, and tortured humanity shedding not words and blood, but words alone?

MELVILLE I told you not to bring that critic crap into this house.

LIZZIE It's from a magazine that you subscribe to.

MELVILLE Cancel the damn subscription... Piece of garbage, the *Atlantic Monthly*... As if they ever publish anything worthwhile...

LIZZIE Well, at least you're making a steady wage.

MELVILLE So after publishing a dozen books I'm supposed to be happy spending the rest of my days as a goddamn Customs Inspector because it's a "steady wage"... Screw them.

LIZZIE Watch your mouth. The children can hear.

MELVILLE I can't believe you're reading that out loud. *(MELVILLE drinks.)*

LIZZIE I thought you might like to know what people are saying about your poetry.

MELVILLE I couldn't give two shits.

LIZZIE Well, I don't think the book's that bad.

MELVILLE I don't care what you think, all right? Or the critics... But I don't have to worry about that anymore, do I? Now that I go to work six days a week.

LIZZIE Well, writing books wasn't any easier for you—

MELVILLE Where's dinner?

LIZZIE It's in the oven.

MELVILLE Is Mackie home?

LIZZIE He went out with some friends.

MELVILLE Again?

LIZZIE With some boys from the militia.

MELVILLE I thought he was going to quit that.

LIZZIE He enjoys it.

MELVILLE I told him not to stay out late anymore.

LIZZIE You did the same thing when you were eighteen.

MELVILLE I just hope he doesn't start developing bad habits.

LIZZIE Mackie doesn't even drink.

MELVILLE He better start listening to what I tell him—

LIZZIE Maybe if you *talked* to him once in a while.

MELVILLE I always talk to him.

LIZZIE You never talk to him. You scream. No wonder he stays out all night.

MELVILLE I only yell when he disobeys.

LIZZIE But he *doesn't* disobey.

MELVILLE I'm going down to the tavern.

LIZZIE So you're not going to have dinner with us?

MELVILLE I'm not about to sit here listening to you all night.

LIZZIE You don't want to listen to anybody.

MELVILLE Not here.

LIZZIE The damn characters in your stories mean more to you than your family.

MELVILLE They're certainly a hell of a lot more interesting.

LIZZIE I'll just feed your pork chops to the dog.

MELVILLE Your food's not even fit for a goddamn dog.

LIZZIE Maybe the drunks will want to listen to your stories.

MELVILLE They're a hell of a lot better company than I get around here.

LIZZIE Maybe your bar buddies can read you all the God-awful reviews about your horrendous poems.

MELVILLE *(MELVILLE raises his hand, screams in her face.)* Shut up!

LIZZIE Don't you ever raise your hand to me—

MELVILLE I told you not to talk about that in here.

LIZZIE Your poetry's shit. All your writing is.

MELVILLE *(MELVILLE grabs her.)* If I hear you say anything like that again, even one more time, I'll kill you. Do you hear me? I'll fucking kill you. *(MELVILLE is EXITING.)*

LIZZIE You just can't deal with anything real. *(BLACKOUT.)*

(Native drumming intensifies. Audience sees video images from schlocky movies that feature South Seas and/or African "natives.")

JAMESON As we pulled away from Nuku Heva a slew of arrows shot towards us, several glancing off the boat's side, but most falling far short, and then six or seven warriors rushed into the sea, hurled their javelins, and began swimming after us. Since we were close to a hundred yards away by then, and just as far from the ship, the chances seemed in our favor. But as the savages quickly gained on us, we realized that we were in one of those choppy, angry seas in which it is so difficult to row. The rowers got out their knives, held them ready between their teeth, and I seized the boat-hook. We were well aware that if the natives succeeded in intercepting us, they would capsize the boat... I discerned Karky closing in on us, his tomahawk between his teeth. *(BLACKOUT. Drumming continues at low volume.)*

Scene Thirty

(Melville home, etc.)

MELVILLE *(MELVILLE knocks on MACKIE's door.)* Mackie... Mackie... Get your ass up, you slothful bastard... Out drinking all night in those uptown dives... Open the door, damn it... Open it... All right... Just be a bum... But you're not going to be a bum in *this* house... I should have given you twenty lashes with the belt. Then your ass would be up and out of bed...

LIZZIE Don't be so harsh on him.

MELVILLE Look what time he came home last night.

LIZZIE He was out having fun with his friends.

MELVILLE He was in a goddamn gin-mill full of dancin' girls and poker games. You good-for-nothin' lout.

LIZZIE Leave him alone.

MELVILLE You can't even answer your father... You big sissy.

LIZZIE *(LIZZIE grabs MELVILLE.)* Stop talking to him like that.

MELVILLE Get offa me! *(MELVILLE pushes LIZZIE to the ground.)*

LIZZIE You... You're a...

MELVILLE If you don't want to answer me, or get up for work, you can stay in there until you rot...

LIZZIE I'm going to call the police.

MELVILLE I didn't—

LIZZIE Pushing your wife to the ground...

MELVILLE I didn't mean to do that... I'm sorry... I just lost my temper because of this damn bastard of a son in here.

LIZZIE *(LIZZIE hits MELVILLE.)* Don't talk to him that way.

MELVILLE *(To LIZZIE, in her face.)* Just get out of here. Out! *(LIZZIE EXITS.)* Listen, you son of a bitch. You better get your ass out of bed, right now. And get to work. And apologize to your mother for getting her all upset. Because if you don't, when I get home from work I'm going to throw your ass out on the street. *(MELVILLE EXITS.)*

Scene Thirty-one

(Split scene: outside MACKIE'S bedroom door; MELVILLE'S office.)

LIZZIE *(Outside MACKIE'S door.)* Mackie... Mackie... Open the door, honey... Are you okay, Mackie?

MELVILLE *(At work, in his office.)* Damn kid... I have to clear a British steamship over on Pier 13... I've got poems to finish... And now I've gotta worry about goddamn Mackie... How the hell am I supposed to write anything... *(MELVILLE works on a poem.)*

LIZZIE Honey...

MELVILLE Art...

In placid hours well-pleased we dream

LIZZIE Mackie...

MELVILLE Of many a brave unbodied scheme...

LIZZIE Just tell me that you're okay.

MELVILLE But form to bend, pulsed life create.

LIZZIE Say something...

MELVILLE What unlike things must meet and hate.

LIZZIE Answer me Mackie.

MELVILLE Hate...

LIZZIE Please, honey.

MELVILLE Instinct and study; love and hate.

LIZZIE You've been in there all day and haven't said a word.

MELVILLE Audacity, *reverence.* These must mate.

LIZZIE Mackie...

MELVILLE And fuse with Jacob's mystic heart.

LIZZIE Just tell me you're awake.

MELVILLE To wrestle...

LIZZIE Please open the door, Mackie.

MELVILLE To wrestle with the Angel...

LIZZIE At least say something...

MELVILLE *(The poem pleases MELVILLE.)* To wrestle with the Angel—Art... *E perfecto*!

LIZZIE Mackie...

(MELVILLE gathers his writings, places them in a briefcase, EXITS. BLACKOUT. LIGHTS UP. MELVILLE ENTERS his home, finds LIZZIE outside of MACKIE'S bedroom door.)

LIZZIE He hasn't come out of his room all day.

MELVILLE He's just sleeping off a drunk.

LIZZIE He wasn't even drinking last night.

MELVILLE His eyes were all bloodshot.

LIZZIE Yes, from crying. Because you kept scolding him and calling him names.

MELVILLE He walked in the door at three o'clock in the morning.

LIZZIE Well, there was no need to yell at him like that.

MELVILLE Somebody's gotta scold him.

LIZZIE And then you started it up all over again this morning.

MELVILLE He's just hungover. He can't handle it... *(MELVILLE begins to EXIT.)*

LIZZIE Where are you going?

MELVILLE Aren't we going to have dinner now?

LIZZIE Dinner?

MELVILLE Yes.

LIZZIE What about your son?

MELVILLE If he can't talk then he can't eat.

LIZZIE He hasn't said a word all day.

MELVILLE I'm going to go work on my writing.

LIZZIE He hasn't even opened the door.

MELVILLE Let him stay locked in there for the rest of the week for all I care.

LIZZIE I just hope he's all right.

MELVILLE What's for dinner?

LIZZIE I haven't made anything.

MELVILLE What?

LIZZIE I've been up here all day knocking on Mackie's door.

MELVILLE Why waste your time on him?

LIZZIE He hasn't spoken. I haven't seen him. I'm worried sick about him.

MELVILLE Maybe he snuck out.

LIZZIE I haven't left the house all day.

MELVILLE *(MELVILLE knocks on the door.)* Mackie! Mackie! Open the door... Open the door, goddamn it! Open it. If you don't open the door right this second, I'm breaking it down, and you're going to pay for a carpenter to come out here and fix it. *(MELVILLE attempts to break the door down.)* Open it, goddamn it! *(MELVILLE breaks down the door. He and LIZZIE ENTER. The rest of the scene takes place off-stage until MELVILLE drags MACKIE'S body on-stage.)*

LIZZIE Oh, my God... Oh, my God. Mackie... Mackie... *(LIZZIE cries.)* Oh, my God... Oh...

MELVILLE I...I...

LIZZIE Oh, my baby...

MELVILLE I...I never thought... Oh, Lord... My son...

LIZZIE Look what you did to him...

MELVILLE Mackie... Son... *(MELVILLE cries.)*

LIZZIE Oh, my God... Look what you did to him.

MELVILLE I didn't mean to... Mackie...

LIZZIE Oh, my baby...

MELVILLE Did...did you hear any gunshots?

LIZZIE No... Mackie...

MELVILLE He couldn't have done this.

LIZZIE Oh, my God... Ohhh...

MELVILLE Someone else must have...

LIZZIE The pistol's still in his hand...

MELVILLE Why would he...

LIZZIE My baby, Mackie... *(MELVILLE drags MACKIE's body, which is covered with sail-cloth, onto the stage. Unbeknownst to audience, MACKIE'S "corpse" is actually a mannequin.)* What are you doing?

MELVILLE He was lying in a pool of blood.

LIZZIE Just leave him be.

MELVILLE But, I...

LIZZIE *(Madly.)* Go get the coroner. *(LIZZIE is crying over body.)*

SCHOLAR *(SCHOLAR ENTERS carrying microphone.)* Thank you very much. Thank you. Let's give the actors a big hand, ladies and gentlemen. *(SCHOLAR claps.)*

LIZZIE We're not finished.

SCHOLAR We're running way behind schedule.

MELVILLE We only need a few more minutes. *(Several actors, upset, speak amongst themselves.)*

SCHOLAR I'm sorry... But several of our conference participants have trains to catch tonight. *(Looks at watch.)* And we're already running half an hour overtime so we really must be finishing up... *(To audience.)* Actually, I would have been out here talking to you sooner...had I walked out onstage earlier... Come on, let's give the actors another rousing round of applause for a job well done. *(SCHOLAR claps. Actors briefly complain amongst themselves, EXIT. The covered corpse remains on stage.)* Well...I'd like to devote my final moments here at the Melvillean Society's annual meeting to my recent...um, uh...discovery...of the undiscovered text I mentioned earlier... To give you a bit of background, Lizzie, Melville's wife, had stored her husband's final manuscript—a masterpiece, it so turns out—in a...a tin...where one stores bread... A bread-tin... The work, a novena...uh, a novella...was recently shown to me by one of Melville's grandaughters, and I offered to edit the manuscript, which wasn't quite complete—because it wasn't finished... The story, entitled *Billy Budd*, takes place on a naval ship where an older, envious sailor falsely and maliciously accuses a handsome teenage sailor, Billy Budd, of treason, and the wrongful accusation leads to the young man's demise. But Billy remains, to the very end, a wholly innocent, saint-like character. This fascinating *tour-de-force*, which *I* discovered, will, I predict, strengthen and solidify my...I mean Melville's reputation as America's greatest author of timeless works on universal themes. And, uh... What the Dickens happened to my last two pages of notes? Oh...I, uh, must have left them backstage... I'll be right back.

(SCHOLAR EXITS. LIGHTS UP on MELVILLE and LIZZIE, who have visibly aged. MELVILLE himself is now 72 years old. Caption reads: THE MELVILLE HOME. NEW YORK CITY, 1891. LIZZIE, who is quite upset, is holding up a manuscript.)

MELVILLE It's just a story.

LIZZIE About a young man. Angelic. Naive. God-like...

MELVILLE No one was supposed to read that.

LIZZIE And Billy Budd's about the same age as Mackie when he—

MELVILLE Billy Budd has absolutely nothing to do with Mackie.

LIZZIE Well, he doesn't commit suicide.

MELVILLE Mackie's death was not a suicide. He was sleeping with a pistol under his pillow.

LIZZIE An older, jealous man's actions lead to Billy's death.

MELVILLE The pistol went off by itself.

LIZZIE A spiteful, unsuccessful man—a sailor—causes a young boy's demise.

MELVILLE Give me that. *(MELVILLE unsuccessfully tries to grab manuscript.)*

LIZZIE Isn't anything sacred to you?

MELVILLE Give it to me.

LIZZIE This is your atonement, isn't it? Your swan song. As if writing yet another story could make up for what you've done.

MELVILLE I told him to get rid of the gun.

LIZZIE What about the eighteen years before Mackie purchased the gun? When you were somewhere else all the time. Locked up in your room day and night because you just had to create "great" American literature. And now Mackie's gone. Dead for twenty-four years. Stanwix died out on the West Coast still a young man, nobody by his side. And not one of your books is even in print anymore. Is that the price of "literature"? Goddamn it, Herman. How could you do this to us? Even if by some miracle somebody is reading your books in the twentieth, the twenty-first century—if your books can even be found by then—what does it really matter? Look at your four children, two of whom are dead at a young age, a third who's an invalid and won't even speak to you anymore... And there's never a day that goes by that I don't think of how Mackie and his brother would still be here today, thriving, with children of their own, if you didn't extract every ounce of life from your own family and stuff it into your goddamn books... You're a cannibal, you know that. Taking poor Mackie's life and using it as fodder for yet another story. *(LIZZIE holds up manuscript.)* If you ever publish this, Herman—even one sentence of it—so help me God, I'll murder you... I will murder you.

MELVILLE Do you know how much time I put into that story you're holding? Over twelve years. I wrote eight novels in less time than that. And you know what? I don't care. I do not care. Take it. Just take it... Throw it into the furnace... Throw everything in the furnace. *(MELVILLE tries not to break down.)*

LIZZIE You expect me to forgive you now, don't you? Well, you know what Herman? No matter how hard I try—and I've tried, believe me. I've prayed for hours upon hours. I've spoken with ministers, friends... But no matter how much I try, I can never, ever forgive you for what you've done... I just hope that the price you extracted from us wasn't completely in vain. *(LIZZIE picks up bread-tin and puts manuscript into it as she EXITS. MELVILLE puts his face into his hands. SCHOLAR ENTERS smiling.)*

Y. MACKIE *(Y. MACKIE remains off-stage during the following sequence or his image appears as a video hologram. His voice is heard at low volume as the SCHOLAR speaks.)* We're full of ghosts and spirits...

SCHOLAR. This discovery of *Billy Budd* is the most important literary find since Aristotle's, ummm...

Y. MACKIE Graveyards full of buried dead that come to life before us, within us.

SCHOLAR Uhhh...Aristotle's *Poetics*...

Y. MACKIE All our dead sires are in us... That's their immortality.

SCHOLAR *(Holds up Billy Budd.)* And I'm delighted to announce that the just printed copies of *Billy Budd*, Melville's greatest work since *Moby-Dick*, are available right now, as I speak, in the hotel's, uh, the place...you know, where you walk in...the, uh...

Y. MACKIE From sire to son, we go on multiplying corpses within ourselves.

SCHOLAR The lobby.

Y. MACKIE Resurrections.

SCHOLAR Oh, uh, and one more thing.

Y. MACKIE Every thought's a soul of some past poet, hero, sage...

SCHOLAR. Let me just find my page here.

Y. MACKIE We're fuller than a city... *(SCHOLAR searches through notes.)*

SCHOLAR Where's my last page of notes? *(SCHOLAR clumsily searches through his papers.)*

Y. MACKIE Woe is it, that reveals these things.

SCHOLAR *(SCHOLAR smiles.)* Excuse me...

(SCHOLAR EXITS. FLANEUR ENTERS with small wooden folding chair, a shoe-shine kit. MELVILLE, still upset, begins to walk, slowly.)

FLANEUR How you doin' there, sir? Have your boots blackened?

MELVILLE No.

FLANEUR I'll give you a good deal, sir.

MELVILLE Why are you constantly following me?

FLANEUR Six cents.

MELVILLE That's too much.

FLANEUR Ain't nobody in Manhattan blackin' boots for six cents...but I'll tell you what. Since you seem like a nice enough gentleman, I'll blacken 'em for five.

MELVILLE Five cents?

FLANEUR *(FLANEUR opens and places on ground wooden folding chair.)* Yes, sir. So if you'll just take a seat.

MELVILLE I'll give you four.

FLANEUR Four cents? Why, that'd barely cover my materials.

MELVILLE Four cents. Take it or leave it.

FLANEUR *(pause)* Have a seat. *(MELVILLE sits. FLANEUR whistles "Dixie" as he sets up equipment, shines.)*

MELVILLE Can you please stop whistling that song.

FLANEUR Why's that, sir?

MELVILLE That's from another time.

FLANEUR Well, I'm from down South.

MELVILLE That...that song connotes divisiveness. Which is something America's still trying to overcome...

FLANEUR I been whistlin' that tune for over twenty-five years.

MELVILLE But it perpetuates social strife.

FLANEUR I never heard that.

MELVILLE Everything that thousands of Union soldiers died for.

FLANEUR It ain't nothin' but a song.

MELVILLE But in whistling that song, you're resurrecting one of the darkest periods of American history, when a certain group of people—

FLANEUR That'll be four cents, sir. *(MELVILLE searches for money.)*

MELVILLE Oh, I, uh... Well, here's two cents... I seem to have forgotten my purse. I must have left it at—

FLANEUR That ain't exactly fair, sir.

MELVILLE I'm sorry. But I...I left the house in a bit of a flurry... Here, why don't you take this book of poems. About the Holy Land.

FLANEUR I don't read poetry.

MELVILLE *(MELVILLE pulls out small bottle of whiskey.)* Well...perhaps I can share some Bushmills with you. *(MELVILLE drinks.)*

FLANEUR I wouldn't mind tastin' a drop or two. *(MELVILLE passes whiskey to FLANEUR.)*

MELVILLE Take a couple of swigs. *(FLANEUR drinks.)*

FLANEUR You got a cigarette?

MELVILLE Sure. *(MELVILLE gives him a cigarette.)* You know, you remind me of a savage with whom I once shared a bed in a New Bedford inn.

FLANEUR Here. *(FLANEUR returns bottle. MELVILLE drinks, returns whiskey to FLANEUR.)*

MELVILLE Before we departed on a whaler together, to the South Seas.

FLANEUR Hmmm... *(FLANEUR drinks.)*

MELVILLE You remind me of a tattoo artist from the Marquesas...of someone I met on Boston Common...in the Pittsfield train station...in the midst of the New